INSIDE PITCH

INSIDE PITCH

Insiders Reveal How the Ill-Fated Seattle Pilots Got Played into Bankruptcy in One Year

RICK ALLEN

PERSISTENCE ERA PRESS

Copyright © 2020 by Rick Allen
All rights reserved.

No part of this book may be reproduced, or stored in a retrieval system, or transmitted in any form or by any means, electronic, mechanical, photocopying, recording, or otherwise, without express written permission of the publisher.

Published by Persistence Press, Tacoma, Washington

Edited and designed by Girl Friday Productions
www.girlfridayproductions.com

Cover design: Paul Barrett
Project management: Sara Spees Addicott
Image credits: cover © Stephen Mcsweeny/Shutterstock

ISBN (paperback): 978-1-7345959-0-1
ISBN (ebook): 978-1-7345959-1-8
Library of Congress Control Number: 2020902141

To my grandchildren, Phoenix, Scarlett, Isla, and Eva: Grandpa has a secret.

CONTENTS

Diminutive Dr. Allen Dictionary of Baseball Semantics ix
Introduction xi

1. Early Signs of a Major League Baseball
   Chief Financial Officer 1
2. Dive Deep, Work Hard, Know How to Play the Game 7
3. Speeding the Transition to a Career in Baseball 11
4. A Seattle Baseball Icon Opens the Door 15
5. Baseball in His Blood 21
6. "Certified Bob" Moves Up 27
7. Welcome to the Big Leagues 35
8. Show Me the Money, Seattle 41
9. A Too-Early Team with Too Many Errors 49
10. Going Nowhere Leads to Going Elsewhere 75
11. Searching for Home Plate 87
12. April Fools' Déjà Vu: New Town,
    New Team, New Problems 99
13. Things Warm Up in Milwaukee 107
14. Deeper Team Depth Buys Milwaukee Time (and More) . . . 133

Epilogue 141
    Bob Schoenbachler 141
    Jim Kittilsby 146
    The Sorianos 147
    Seattle Baseball 148
    Bud Selig 150
Acknowledgments 153
Notes 157
About the Author 163

DIMINUTIVE DR. ALLEN
DICTIONARY OF BASEBALL SEMANTICS

Inside pitch *noun*

1: a pitch thrown over the inside part of the plate, often intended to make contact with the ball more difficult for the batter

2: also known as a "high hard one," thrown with intent, dangerously close to the opponent to surprise, disrupt, or startle

3: an argument or proposition made to a group by one member, often giving the presenter an edge in decision-making that may affect others outside of the group

INTRODUCTION

Bob Schoenbachler only played sandlot baseball in the Kent Valley south of Seattle. He was cut from his high school team before playing an inning. But at the ripe old age of nineteen, he found himself keeping the books for a AAA Seattle baseball team and hanging out with Jimmie Reese, Babe Ruth's only roommate, who, in the process, introduced Bob to Warren Spahn, arguably the best left-handed pitcher to ever play the game. And all of this before Bob Schoenbachler ever saw a live major league game.

In a relatively short time, Bob would find himself named the comptroller of the newly formed 1969 Seattle Pilots Major League Baseball (MLB) team, the only team in MLB history to go bankrupt after one year and be spirited off to another city. The bankruptcy wasn't because of Bob's youth and inexperience as a twenty-one-year-old comptroller, but we'll get to that dizzy journey shortly.

Bob's quick ascent to a key position on a major league team was only the beginning of a truth-is-stranger-than-fiction meteoric rise and adventure as a twentysomething trusted insider. He was in possession of such sensitive financial information that he could have easily ended up testifying in court if anything went awry . . . which, in fact, it did.

Meanwhile, Jim Kittilsby was seemingly born to baseball. A good shortstop in his hometown of Kalispell, Montana, he was good enough to play college ball as an outfielder at

Pacific Lutheran University in Tacoma, Washington. Unlike Bob Schoenbachler, with his unlikely path to the Seattle Pilots, Kittilsby was on an intentional baseball beeline. After administrative stints with both AAA and major league teams, he arrived as a twenty-nine-year-old administrator with the Pilots, coming over from the San Francisco Giants, with baseball in his blood.

As a Pilots administrator, within months Jim Kittilsby was loaded with multiple titles and responsibilities as a result of crazy goings-on behind the scenes with the Pilots, as well as Jim's well-earned reputation as a "get it done" baseball guy.

During their careers in the game in Seattle and later in the early transition to Milwaukee, both Bob and Jim dealt with everything from crazy to crazy-like-a-fox general managers, wily and wobbly major league owners, quirky and not-so-quick midlevel counterparts, and other so-called leaders in MLB ownership, at least one apparently so drunk that he could barely stand.

Ball Four, the infamous and groundbreaking book by pitcher Jim Bouton, revealed the startling behind-the-curtain truth of the lives of baseball players on the 1969 Seattle Pilots and other teams. It broke barriers and shook the foundation of the game. Ironically, which very young Seattle Pilots administrator was asked by Jim Bouton in 1969 to unknowingly mimeograph copies of *Ball Four* as it was being written? Yep. Bob Schoenbachler.

Inside Pitch reveals insider secrets on the administrative side of the game during the same era, and in fact, with the very same team: the one-year-wonder 1969 Seattle Pilots.

Who do you think was observing their own peers and often bumbling sidekicks as young men of twenty-one and twenty-nine suddenly hoisted into major positions in Major League Baseball at a critical time in the evolution of the game? Bob Schoenbachler and Jim Kittilsby.

And who ended up moving to Milwaukee and working for that new team when the Pilots were sold out from under Seattle during spring training 1970? Again, Bob Schoenbachler and Jim Kittilsby. Both Bob and Jim made the transition to the start-up 1970 Milwaukee Brewers, a new team with its own set of surprising administrative eye-openers, also chronicled here.

Who ended up alone in Tempe, Arizona, in April 1970, closing down the last remnants of the Pilots and simultaneously taking instructions from the bankruptcy court in Seattle as well as Milwaukee attorneys while trying to get into his padlocked offices? Jim Kittilsby.

Who worked as new Milwaukee owner Bud Selig's finance guy and watched as Selig's Ford dealership purchased tickets to give away and keep people in the bleachers as attendance plummeted in the early years after the 1970 transition to Milwaukee? Bob Schoenbachler.

And who ended up as the commissioner of baseball several years later? Nope, not Bob. Not Jim. But Bud Selig, their Milwaukee boss, did.

Owners, general managers, and assistant GMs, public relations guys, minor-league administrators, team lawyers, and even secretaries (the title used at the time)—none should be digging in at the plate for a comfortable at-bat as they read through this book. A high hard one is about to whiz by a few ears as Bob Schoenbachler and his administrative cohort Jim Kittilsby dust off remarkable memories to reveal stunning insider secrets from fifty years ago.

To baseball fans, though, *Inside Pitch* will help to close out a complete game. Bob and Jim reveal funny facts and surprising inside stories about the not-so-smooth administrative functioning of America's pastime with the one-year Seattle Pilots and then the start-up Milwaukee Brewers.

Take a road trip back in time and read some hilarious new insights on why the Pilots floundered their way into bankruptcy in a single season and headed east for Milwaukee in the spring of 1970.

1

Early Signs of a Major League Baseball Chief Financial Officer

Bob Schoenbachler was born in 1947, the year Major League Baseball was finally integrated and Jackie Robinson suited up for the Dodgers.

Bob grew up in the Kent Valley south of Seattle in Washington State. At the time, and into the late 1950s, the fields of the valley, which more recently held much of Boeing, the multinational airplane manufacturing company, were fertile land, sweeping tracts of agriculture and smaller family farms. The fields were worked by Filipinos, Japanese, and Mexicans, both adults and kids. Anglo kids often worked alongside them on the farms owned by their families. Workers, parents, and kids alike shared a strong work ethic fueled by a survival instinct developed during World War II, an ethic that was helping America become a world leader in the precomputer age as the rest of the world was in recovery.

Bob's first memory of baseball was the thrill of going to a Seattle Rainiers minor league game—a thrill because, at the time, it wasn't an easy trek from rural farmland to Seattle for Bob or most of his friends. The 15 miles might as well have been 150 given the time it took to traverse mostly two-lane back roads from rural farmland to the Big City. It was a trip no farm boy made often.

Neither did competing in organized league baseball happen often for many of the same kids. Little League, founded in 1939, right before World War II, and with slow growth during the war, was a big leap. Organized leagues were few and far between in more rural areas. The time it took, and the transportation required, to get to a league was a sacrifice most rural families, including Bob's, couldn't make. Working the farm, plowing the fields, maintaining the tractors, cleaning the barns, fixing the machinery, and for some, milking the cows, were by necessity higher priorities. Bob's instinct was to learn as much as possible about as many jobs as there were on his farm. Organized baseball took a back seat. Youth baseball for Bob consisted mostly of sandlot pickup games. Filipino and Anglo kids chose sides and played each other, almost always without fights or petty bickering.

Japanese and Mexican families also lived in the area, but the Japanese families, having been in internment camps from 1942 to 1945, were still in the long process of starting over from scratch, and most of the kids were younger than Bob, who was on the very front edge of the "baby boom." One can speculate that many of the Japanese couples, while they were integrating into the farming community, waited a few years longer after the war to add to their families, until they got back on their feet economically. The Mexican families were fewer at the time.

In any event, most who participated both in the fields and on the ballfield found a way to work together, all having more in common than they had differences. "Thinking back," Bob relates, "we didn't even see differences; we shared common experiences." This "work and play together" approach likely influenced a big part of Bob's later success, both in baseball administration at the highest levels and in his life after baseball.

Bob had a lingering interest in baseball as he entered O'Dea High School, a Seattle Catholic school. He tried out for the team there in his first year, but didn't make it past the last cut, being one of the last to be told, "Not this year." Bob was disappointed, but not heartbroken. He wasn't at all a baseball fanatic. And he wasn't at O'Dea long enough to give it another try.

During his O'Dea days, Bob's entrepreneurial instincts and natural talent for accounting began to show themselves, albeit in curious ways. Bob led the informal group interested in "lagging coins," seeing who could loft a coin from a given point and land it closest to the wall . . . winner take all.

He was also an instigator of the group that played three-person heads or tails, with coins tossed in the air, caught, and slapped on top of the opposite hand. The odd man with the single head or tail showing on his coin again won it all.

Bob was learning lots at school; it just wasn't always part of the formal curriculum. One thing he learned was that he liked making money and closely keeping track of it.

It wasn't long before his approach to making money began to get a bit more sophisticated. He found small plastic breath-freshener spray bottles at the drug store for something like nineteen cents apiece. He'd take off the tops and replace the liquid with vodka lifted from his dad's stash. He sold the liquored-up plastic spray bottles to insider friends at school who hung out with him. Turning a tidy profit, this was among the first signs of his aptitude in what would become an unlikely career as a finance guy moving money in a much bigger game.

This most lucrative venture, the vodka-filled containers, went belly up when one of his classmate customers broke a rule Bob himself had imposed: never take out the spray container in class. Perhaps in a show of teenage independence or defiance, he decided to freshen up during class . . . a class in which Bob was also a student. The Catholic brother teaching the class caught the act.

"What is that?" the brother inquired. Bob's rule-breaker replied simply, "A spray for my breath." The brother demanded the small container; he sprayed the liquid on his wrist and smelled it. "Where did you get this?" he demanded. The classmate slowly turned in his seat and in feigned innocence pointed at Bob Schoenbachler. "He gave it to me."

"Where did you get this?" the brother demanded of Bob while holding the container aloft for all to see.

Not wanting to lie (he was, after all, in Catholic school), Bob did the only thing he felt he could: he told the truth. "At the drug store," he said with a shrug. Not a lie at all; but certainly not the answer the brother sought.

Unable to immediately remove the top from the spray container to get at its contents (a trick Bob had mastered through trial and error), the brother simply turned, put the container on his desk, and suggested that "more may come of this later." It never did, although according to the school rumor mill the drug-store owner was subsequently questioned about selling liquor to minors. No one knows for sure.

Surprisingly, it was none of his entrepreneurial adventures that shortened Bob's O'Dea career and prevented him from giving baseball another try. He was always sufficiently discreet (a characteristic that served him especially well in Major League Baseball circles) that none of those issues were raised to the level of extreme administrative discontent or disciplinary action. His days at O'Dea, and his last shot at playing baseball in high school, came to an abrupt end because he refused to play the trumpet.

New braces on his teeth were cutting into his lips. He couldn't hold a note, wasn't enjoying the experience, and didn't want to negatively impact the performance of the other students.

"I'm going to drop band class and stop playing," Bob told the brother conducting the class. The brother's reply startled him, partly because he had previously been so nice and encouraging. He had a reputation of being particularly friendly to students. "You better show up tomorrow and you better play . . . or you'll pay a price," the brother warned.

Bob showed up to school the next day but, despite the warning, didn't attend band class after school. The following day, the brother entered one of Bob's classes, called him into the hallway, shoved him against the wall, and hit him in the chest with his fist. "You *will* play," the brother threatened. Bob responded in kind, "No, I won't." And instinctively, he hit the brother back.

End of career at O'Dea, but not before he found all of his grades lowered a full grade as punishment for his fighting back against a brother.

In a "what goes around comes around" moment many years later, Bob remembers that his suddenly angry Catholic brother nemesis was among a number of administrators and clergy to be accused of sexually exploiting minors at school. The archdiocese in Seattle eventually agreed to a multimillion-dollar settlement involving many cases, including those at O'Dea, dating back to the early 1960s.

2

Dive Deep, Work Hard, Know How to Play the Game

Bob's transition out of O'Dea was eased by turning his attention to other things: girls and cars, with cars taking the lead. Schoenbachler's dad accelerated his son's passion for automobiles by offering to match every dollar he earned by his sixteenth birthday so he could buy a car. His father's inducement affirmed and reinforced Bob's strong and focused work ethic, qualities that later would be noticed by important people in the baseball business.

At fourteen years old, Bob obtained a job as a busboy at the Hyatt House on Highway 99 by the Seattle-Tacoma International Airport. But by his sixteenth birthday, he had parlayed that opportunity into work as a valet, as a receptionist, in the laundry, as a waiter (where he learned a thing or two from a good-looking older "waitress" named Rosie who made sure special customers got special attention), and even in the kitchen helping with catered events. He wanted to learn every aspect of the business, just as he did on the farm. Whatever job (and money) was available, he took. He made a few nice tips from Rosie herself, when he discreetly pointed out customers looking for a bit more than a good night's sleep at the Hyatt.

Once again, Bob's natural entrepreneurial instincts and ability to handle sensitive data discreetly—skills that, as we shall see, would serve him well in baseball—were instrumental in his success on the job at a very young age.

Just his luck, the Hyatt House burned to the ground about a year after he started there. But his reputation as a hard worker, quick learner, and person of discretion apparently paid off, because within a few short weeks he received a call from the Holiday Inn offering him a job. He hadn't even applied, but some of his coworkers had earlier made the transition to there. He was quickly back in the saddle at the Holiday Inn, working on-the-side catering events for which many of the waitresses had recommended him.

By the time he turned sixteen, he had saved enough, with his father's match, to buy his first car. It was a brand-new maroon 1964 Chevrolet Impala Super Sport with a 327 engine and a four-speed transmission. The interior was solid black with chrome trim, with bucket seats and a full black-and-chrome console down the middle.

Next thing you know, Bob took a second job at a gas station, where they allowed him to work around his school and Holiday Inn schedule. He used the lift bays and other equipment to work on his car when not serving customers. He studied car engines inside and out and learned details of every major component, enabling him to make revisions on the Impala to increase the horsepower. Loving speed, he started drag racing at the local tracks. And thus began a love affair with cars and speed that nearly killed him . . . an event that, had it happened, would have permanently scuttled his later career as a major league accounting executive. But we'll get to that misadventure, and how it actually accelerated his baseball career, shortly.

In the meantime, while Bob was finishing up at a public high school, he found himself enjoying business and the detail of accounting classes. He graduated from high school in 1965 and decided to pursue his "making money" interest by taking accounting at Highline, a community college situated between Seattle to the north and Tacoma to the south, not far from his home in Kent. Having worked every from-the-ground-up job in two different hotels, Bob was imagining himself in hotel and motel management . . . quite a distance from a major league baseball CFO. Baseball wasn't anywhere on his agenda.

3

Speeding the Transition to a Career in Baseball

Two things interrupted Bob's Highline Community College adventure, which lasted about as long as his experience at O'Dea High School. The first was his affinity for racing and speed, where doubling down on speed and nearly killing himself comes in.

Just before his high school graduation, Bob had traded in his hopped-up '64 Impala Super Sport for a 1962 Corvette . . . a lot more car, and a lot faster, in a smaller package. It was a teenager's dream, especially a teenager with an affinity for speed.

Several weeks after graduation, Bob was to attend the birthday party of his best friend at a local beach and get in some water skiing. In a hurry to get there and having had a few early libations to make the occasion especially happy, Bob was following his friend at somewhere near double the speed limit on some back roads near his home, enjoying the power of his "new" '62 Corvette with an open case of beer in the front seat. While his memory isn't perfectly clear, he suspects it was either Olympia or Rainier beer, Northwest favorites.

The memory isn't perfectly clear because as Bob's friend came to a curve too fast and slammed on his brakes, Bob did the same, and he lost control. His treasured Corvette slammed into a telephone pole, rebounded off it, wheels still spinning, and slammed into it again, bending the entire body of the car. Parts of the car ended up nearly in Bob's lap, trapping him in the front seat, with one leg particularly damaged. Tendons, nerves, and muscle were all cut, and an artery was almost hit, which would have proven fatal. Trapped in the front seat as his friend rushed back to the totaled Corvette, Bob remembers one thing clearly . . . telling his friend to get the case of beer the hell out of the car.

Emergency workers used special tools to pry Schoenbachler out from behind what was left of the wheel. They rapidly treated the wounds in his legs. He spent three weeks in the hospital. Much closer to death than anyone knew, Bob was lucky to have survived. He had kept it secret from his friends that he was a hemophiliac, prone to bleeding, most often in the joints.

Dr. DeMarsh, a "fantastic doctor," had discreetly arranged for Bob to obtain needed blood transfusions at a local blood bank during his youth. The doctor had encouraged him to be open about his condition, but instead Bob hid it for years. Dr. DeMarsh, Bob said, "treated me like an adult all the time and was very straight with me. He didn't pull punches. He was a great mentor when I needed one as a headstrong kid."

It was Dr. DeMarsh who warned him to be careful with his knees while still encouraging him to play sports. As the doctor once told him: "Don't worry; you can do lots of other things in sports." As future events would prove, Dr. DeMarsh was on the mark more than he could have imagined.

After the crash in his Corvette and his release from the hospital, Bob got out his crutches from previous injuries and enrolled at Highline.

At Highline Community College and on the mend, Schoenbachler's path took another turn. His own admitted lack of patience, an unwillingness to go through all the required (and what he considered "boring and unnecessary") college courses, prompted an early exit. With his slowly healing legs in great pain, he dropped out in 1966.

Little did he know at the time that speeding around a corner, then a detour in his education, were the turning points that would lead him to starting an early career in Major League Baseball.

4

A Seattle Baseball Icon Opens the Door

Edo Vanni was a baseball icon in Seattle, playing, coaching, managing, or otherwise working for every professional team in Seattle except the Seattle Mariners (who gave him lifetime tickets and a parking space). Edo was known as the "Dean of Baseball" in Seattle.[1]

As a senior at Seattle's Queen Anne High School in 1937, Vanni, a pretty diminutive guy by today's standards for a star athlete at about 5' 7", was an all-city selection in football and baseball. He earned scholarships to the University of Washington, but after a solid year as quarterback on the freshman team, he was signed by the Seattle Rainiers minor league baseball team, where he batted .301, .325, and .333 in his first three professional seasons. Injuries and World War II got in the way after that. On his return after the war, he eventually moved to management and the administrative side.

Everyone in the game loved Edo except opponents, because, as his wife was apparently fond of saying, "He could start a fight in an empty room." It was reported that Vanni endeared himself to Seattle Rainiers minor league baseball fans "by trading fisticuffs over the smallest slight, and it didn't matter who or how big the opponent was."[2]

In Vanni's own words, accompanied by a chuckle: "I started about thirty fights one year. That was my job—stir up the ball club."[3]

In Seattle he was once ejected before the game even started for bringing a friend's St. Bernard as a seeing-eye dog to home plate while delivering the lineup card, a comment on his disputes with umpires the previous night.[4]

Over his many years in the game, Edo apparently kept a sharp eye out for hard workers who might be interested in a baseball career and made himself available as a mentor to them. In 1968, he even sent a telegram to the 1955 batboy of the Seattle Rainiers, Jim Johnson, asking if he would be interested in a public relations position with the fledgling Seattle major league team. Said Johnson, "I was in a successful new career in insurance and had just won a sales award in the business; shortly after, I was stunned to receive the only wire of my life, from Edo Vanni, asking if I'd be interested in working for what became the Seattle Pilots. I'd worked as a batboy for the AAA Rainiers in 1955 in Sick's Stadium thirteen years earlier and had a great time doing it. Edo is the guy who hired me then, and it was both a surprise and honor to be contacted so many years later. But I had to turn him down, as my business career was taking off."

Now, just a year earlier than the wire to Johnson, here was Edo Vanni, a hugely popular general manager of the now AAA-level Seattle Angels, staring at a nineteen-year-old kid dressed in his Sunday best, perhaps interested in a baseball career.

Edo Vanni, "Dean of Seattle baseball" as a Seattle Rainiers player (left) and as a Seattle Pilots administrator (right). (Source: Private Collection [left]; MOHAI, Seattle Post-Intelligencer Collection, 2000.107.219.21.01 [right])

Bob was standing in Edo's office doorway, applying for the open auditor position with the Seattle Angels in 1967, about to interview with a guy he knew little to nothing about. Bob had just happened to see the job opening posted on a bulletin board and decided to apply.

"I remember Edo's first words were simple, just 'Take a seat,'" Bob recalled. "Then he joked around a bit; he was trying hard to put me at ease."

Fortunately for Bob, Edo was hiring someone for his own team; he was much easier on teammates than opponents. Bob didn't know this, of course. But Bob also didn't know at the time that he was talking with a Seattle baseball icon.

It was Bob's very first professional job interview outside of the hotel industry. Many of his other work experiences were based on taking what was available when no one else stepped up, or because he was recommended for catering events and was asked to work them.

The interview lasted about forty-five minutes, most of it casual learning on the part of both Bob and Edo. Bob remembers one question that was something like, "Where do you see yourself in the future?"

And he remembers his response: "I suspect I'll be going wherever accounting takes me," not realizing at the time how accurate that statement would become in his about-to-blossom career as an insider in professional baseball administration.

His interest in accounting, but not in the required nonaccounting courses he found irrelevant, had already taken him out of Highline Community College following his accident. The accident injuries had also limited his ability to continue with hotel work. Bad knees and a bad back limited his ability to fill the jack-of-all-trades roles he used to volunteer for continuously. So, Bob had immediately followed accounting to Peterson Business School, where the required courses were more relevant to his interests. The bulk of his courses were now accounting, which he was growing to love.

His success in Peterson Business School first led Bob to a private accounting job as part of an internship facilitated by the school placement office. As Bob recalls, "That was a terrible job; the guy worked out of his home, so that's where I worked, too. He would yell at and hit his kids and wife, and I just couldn't take it, so I quit. And that's why I walked back into the school placement office in early 1967, where I just happened to see the ad posted on the board for a finance-related opening with the Seattle AAA baseball team. Having just quit a job I hated but needed, my first thought was 'Well, it's worth a try.' And I liked baseball."

Bob thought the interview with Edo, "a really friendly guy," went well. But having not gone through this formal a process before, especially in the professional baseball world, he didn't know what to expect next.

After hearing nothing for a few days, his mind began to wander back to the idea of another job search and interview.

But on day four, Edo called and asked Bob to come in for further discussion.

This time Edo laid out in more detail what the job might involve. Questioning got around to what part of the job description interested Bob the most. Having had experience as a jack-of-all-trades and having seen how that served him well in multiple other jobs and ways, Bob's response was "All of it. And I'd want to learn everything I can about the entire organization; I want to understand how everything works and how it relates to the budget, costs, and revenue."

Vanni liked that answer. "He was all in favor of me working in the concessions, in the ticket office, checking the stands during the game, and whatever else I thought might be adding to my understanding of money management for the team."

So that is how, on February 13, 1967, nineteen-year-old Bob Schoenbachler was given an intentional walk to first base as auditor of the Seattle Angels, the AAA ball club of the major league California Angels. Admittedly wet behind the ears and with no accounting degree, he started at a salary of four hundred dollars a month on a twelve-month contract.

Vanni told Schoenbachler that he could continue his schooling and pursue other interests in the off-season's slower winter months. But things never slowed down, an early sign of the nature of his career as a baseball administrator. He continued attending night school, eventually obtaining his degree in accounting from Peterson.

He had no idea that in a span of about thirty-six months, his accounting job would expand to include increasing responsibilities; first, for the AAA Angels, next a newly independent and unaffiliated AAA minor league club in Seattle, then for a new major league club in Seattle named the Pilots . . . and then for a second new major league club, requiring a move to a city a thousand miles away.

Nor could he have imagined in his wildest dreams that his future boss would be Bud Selig, who would eventually become the commissioner of all Major League Baseball.

5

Baseball in His Blood

While Bob Schoenbachler's path to baseball was filled with curves and change-ups, Jim Kittilsby, by contrast, pretty much got there on a fastball.

Kittilsby distinguished himself as a very good American Legion shortstop in Kalispell, Montana, despite the region's lack of opportunity for the sport (there hasn't been baseball in Montana high schools since 1947). He was good enough to play the outfield in college ball at Pacific Lutheran University in Tacoma. He loved the game.

As much as he loved playing, he was realistic about his capabilities. He knew that if he was to continue in the game, it wouldn't be as a player at any higher levels. He was aware of the talent around him, and recognized that he had reached the limits of his physical abilities in baseball. So, in the fall of his senior year at Pacific Lutheran, he made the transition from player to administrator.

At the age of twenty-one, Jim took a job with the local AAA Tacoma Giants, farm club to the San Francisco Giants at the time. They were located just a short distance from Pacific

Lutheran University. Today, ironically, they are the AAA team affiliated with the Seattle Mariners.

And here is where a number of fortunate connections set Jim up for a series of further transitions. Those connections eventually landed him with the 1969 Seattle Pilots as a "seasoned administrator" at the age of twenty-nine.

Hired as assistant ticket manager with Tacoma in 1960, Kittilsby found Lew Matlin, business manager, to be a good boss and great first mentor in the professional game. "To this day I remember Lew's early words to me after he hired me: 'Don't put on the swells.' What he meant was, don't let working for a AAA team right off the bat go to your head; keep your eyes and ears open and your nose to the grindstone, and do the work that needs to be done. That advice served me well, and especially well when I dropped into the chaos of the Seattle Pilots a few years later."

Being in Tacoma in 1960 paid off in other ways for Jim. In fact, it's where he had his first introduction to Max Soriano, brother to Dewey Soriano, a former Seattle Rainiers pitcher prior to World War II and a Pacific Coast League executive who would later purchase the major league franchise that became the Seattle Pilots. "Max would occasionally drive down to Tacoma from Seattle and help with the phones in the ticket office, so we became acquainted then; he was a good guy, a hard worker, learning the game himself from the ground up."

Max, a maritime attorney, later represented the Pilots, working with older brother Dewey. Jim would, after gathering a few years and a few teams under his belt, eventually meet up with Max again.

In addition to the above important administrative contacts, the 1960 Tacoma AAA team was filled with some of the best young players in the game, as well as an older player who was a near icon. The team briefly included later Hall of Fame pitchers Juan Marichal and Gaylord Perry, as well as later Hall of Fame hitter Willie McCovey, in addition to Matty Alou, one of the three Alou brothers to later famously play in the same outfield with San Francisco. All on the Tacoma team were only twenty-two years old.

Dusty Rhodes, the hitting hero of the New York Giants in the 1954 World Series, was also on that team, nearing the end of his career. Rhodes was called "the best pinch hitter I've ever seen" by famous player and manager Leo Durocher.

"I got to know a few of the players by paying attention to their interests and needs, and occasionally running errands. The one I remember best was when Gaylord Perry hurt his foot. In Phoenix during spring training, I drove him in my car to the podiatrist. Establishing a good rapport with players always remained important to me."

Kittilsby continued with Tacoma for two years, obtaining experience in multiple roles, through the 1961 season. That year the team won ninety-seven games, came in first in the Pacific Coast League, and drew attendance of nearly a quarter of a million fans, a very good number for a minor league team then. That success helped make Kittilsby's resume look quite nice. As a result, Jim was offered and accepted a higher position, that of business manager with AAA Salt Lake City, a Chicago Cubs affiliate. He moved to Salt Lake City and stayed there for the 1962, 1963, and 1964 seasons.

In 1965, Jim took the same business manager position in a return to the Northwest and the Tacoma Giants, replacing his friend and mentor Lew Matlin, who was named general manager of the Hawaii Islanders.

Jim wasn't aware of how short this reunion with Tacoma would be.

The Giants would move the AAA franchise to Phoenix in late 1965, and he would follow. But that would only happen after he found himself as the last person at the Tacoma stadium, charged with closing it down. He slept on a cot in the stadium, an experience that would serve him especially well in his final days with the infamous Seattle Pilots a few years later.

After spending 1966 with the San Francisco Giants AAA team in Phoenix, Jim was offered a position with the San Francisco major league club, where he worked in a variety of roles during the 1967 season. It was there that he reconnected with Max Soriano, this time via a phone call from Max late in the season.

"Would you be interested in returning to the Northwest and working with us next year as we prepare for the start-up of the new Seattle major league team?" Max queried. He and brother Dewey had arranged to purchase the AAA Seattle Angels, with an eye on preparing the team for a transition into Major League Baseball. They were assembling a management team.

Kittilsby jumped at the offer. He knew that Horace Stoneham, San Francisco owner, was facing some financial difficulty and was soon to face additional competition from a new team that Charlie Finley was moving from Kansas City to Oakland just across the bay. Kittilsby thought the Seattle offer would more likely be financially secure. And the job put him just up the road from his alma mater, Pacific Lutheran University, and the city where he took his first professional job in the game with AAA Tacoma.

January 1968 marked Kittilsby's first month on the new job, and about the end of Bob Schoenbachler's first year with the same Seattle team. Twenty-nine-year-old Kittilsby showed up in the parking lot at Seattle's Sick's Stadium excited to help transition a now-independent AAA Seattle team in 1968 to a major league team in 1969. He was the new business manager, a title that would be expanded several times, with additional responsibilities, in the coming months.

Perhaps an ominous sign of things to come, Seattle general manager Edo Vanni didn't even know Kittilsby had been hired.

"Hell, we don't need another administrator," he said upon learning that Kittilsby would be a direct report. "I need a damn left-handed pitcher." It was tongue in cheek, but Vanni's focus never wavered: he wanted to win on the field.

Meeting Jim in the parking lot that first day was the twenty-year-old auditor of the AAA Seattle team, Bob Schoenbachler.

Bob at that time knew a lot more about the financial condition of the Seattle team, which was no better, and likely worse, than that of the San Francisco team Jim was leaving. Together with other staff during 1968, and particularly in 1969 with the new Pilots, they would have their eyes opened a lot wider as they battled for survival of the franchise.

But for now, the "transition AAA team" owned by the Sorianos in 1968 was optimistically and out of necessity staffing up. And Bob and Jim would be on their way to a friendship that would last more than fifty years. They would also be on their way to jointly experiencing some jaw-dropping administrative funny business in a chaotic battle to save a fledgling Major League Baseball team in Seattle.

Left: Dewey Soriano (seated) with Seattle Rainiers manager Fred Hutchinson, circa 1955. Soriano was selected as 1955 Minor League Executive of the Year by the Sporting News. This was also the year Edo Vanni hired batboy Jim Johnson, whom thirteen years later Edo tried to hire to work for the new Seattle Pilots. Right: Max Soriano (right) accepts a novelty key from Seattle mayor Dorm Braman outside Sicks Stadium, 1969. (Source: David Eskenazi Collection)

6

"Certified Bob" Moves Up

As it turns out, the accounting books for the minor league Seattle AAA team, which was still affiliated with the California Angels in 1967, were in pretty bad shape when Bob Schoenbachler started his new position.

"Let's just say that 'minor league' applied to a lot more than just the baseball players," he recalled.

Jean Fisher was filling the bookkeeper role for the AAA Seattle Angels as best she could with a limited background in accounting. She was also Edo Vanni's secretary, making her just a part-time bookkeeper. Her husband, Ted, was the groundskeeper for the team. If it sounds a little like a "mom and pop shop," Bob said, smiling, "it's because it was."

"I'd say Jean was the queen bee at the time," recalls Bob. "You didn't want to cross her, she knew a lot, and she was nice, so I tread lightly."

"I couldn't figure out the books right from the start, her filing system didn't make any sense to anyone but her," Bob remembers. "They were never right. Jean was a really nice lady, she knew where everything was in her head, and she knew everybody, but she was out of her league in that bookkeeping job as far as formal accounting goes."

Bob went to work on the books, and to him that meant going to work on everything related to the books. He worked the concession stand for a time to learn the ropes there; he worked in the ticket office to see how things were handled and how the money made its way into the books he was trying to understand. Bob was in "dive deep and learn the ropes" mode, which he had applied to most every other job in his past. And just as business manager Lew Matlin had once advised Jim Kittilsby to do, Schoenbachler kept his eyes and ears open and his nose to the grindstone, doing the work that needed to be done.

Bill Sears, assistant to the general manager for public relations and promotion, and highly respected marketing guy, came up with a branding nickname for Bob. Based on his attention to every detail at the ballpark relating to costs, revenue, accounting, and the books, and his intent to do it right, "Certified Bob" was fast establishing himself as a pro and being recognized for it.

"Bill Sears was one of the first staff members I met. Like Edo, he had a constant smile. He was very articulate, and the dark-rimmed glasses he wore gave him an air of confidence and importance. He, like Edo did, joked around with me and made me feel part of the team. And he had a real talent for quickly sizing people up with accuracy."

Having worked the Seattle sports scene since the 1950s, Sears was highly regarded, often described as "diligent, creative, and resourceful." He was also not one to get overly flustered. He could maintain a sense of balance and a sense of humor, according to both Schoenbachler and Kittilsby. "Even though the Sorianos hired several staff from contacts in the Pacific Coast League and elsewhere in baseball, they missed on several they hired," Schoenbachler said, and Kittilsby agreed.

"But Bill Sears was a definite asset, and a local guy who was highly respected," Kittilsby emphasized.

Sears's balance and calmness had probably also contributed to his success in the Army Air Corps in World War II. He was a waist gunner in a B-17 bomber and flew thirty-five missions over Europe. Flight crew workers once counted 350 bullet holes in his plane after he returned from a mission. If history tells us anything, it is that such missions were never without great danger. Getting through them took a steady hand and head, and a lot of luck.

Reporter Dan Raley described Sears this way in a 2007 article in the *Seattle Post-Intelligencer* newspaper: "It was this resourcefulness for four decades that endeared Sears to a lengthy list of teams and other suitors, and made him a press favorite."[1]

Bill Sears, from Seattle Pilots brochure. *(Courtesy of Chris McKinney)*

In addition to Sears, twenty-year-old Certified Bob continued working with General Manager Edo Vanni. This enabled him to get to know the players, learn about contracts and player movement up and down in the system, and the impact of all these machinations on costs.

"Edo would do anything for a laugh . . . he was crazy, funnier than hell. He kept everyone entertained. He reminded me of Bob Uecker, who later was the announcer for the Milwaukee Brewers and a professional comedian who appeared in movies.

"Edo decided that I needed to have some experience selling season tickets, so he gave me a list of contacts. So out I went. I ended up one day in Smith Tower in downtown Seattle, with a businessman who hadn't renewed his season tickets. This was all pretty new to me and I was nervous, but went into my sales pitch anyway. Suddenly the guy leans over, opens a drawer on his desk, and pulls out a clunky wooden contraption with moving parts and a handle that moved all the parts as it turned. He kept turning it as I was talking, so I finally stopped with the sales pitch and asked, 'What is that thing?' 'It's a bullshit grinder, and I'm clearing the area,' he responded. To this day, I think Edo set me up for that one. I can't remember if the guy renewed his tickets or not, but it was worth a good laugh. Years later I told the players on a ball team I coached the funny story about it; one of them found one in a secondhand store, so I now have a picture of it."

The "bullshit grinder" (Courtesy of Bob Schoenbachler)

Quietly, young Bob Schoenbachler was becoming "one of the guys."

"We used to go to Gasperetti's restaurant, where Bill Gasperetti, Bill Sears, Edo Vanni, and I would hang out, eat lots of spaghetti and drink lots of wine [notably, the drinking age at the time was twenty-one, which apparently didn't apply if you were one of the guys; Bob was twenty]. They were always giving me a bunch of shit, calling me Certified Bob and making fun of me for digging into all the detail. But I knew they appreciated the effort I was making and the fact I was straightening things out in accounting."

That being said, Vanni could still come down hard when things didn't go right. "I really screwed up once with a player that Edo was sending down from AAA to AA in the middle of the year. I think his name was Murphy, but don't remember for sure. Anyway, I happened to see Murphy with his head down right outside Edo's office. So, I said in my most sensitive voice something like, 'Hey, Murph, really sorry to hear you're going down.' Trouble was, he hadn't been in Edo's office yet and didn't have a clue.

"I really got my rear end chewed out for that one. One of Edo's favorite phrases was 'That guy could screw up a one-car funeral.' I suspect he might have been thinking that very thing about me on that day."

Bob also started hanging out with one of the coaches in that first year, Jimmie Reese, an old-timer base coach and also known to this day as the best fungo hitter in all of baseball. "You could tell he enjoyed being around the younger players. He would hit grounders to the infielders using his special fungo bat, split in half with tape around it. He was so accurate with that bat that when I stood in the dugout holding a glove up, he could hit a ball to me from home plate and I didn't even have to move my glove!"

A slender six feet tall, sixty-six years old at the time, "and always well dressed" according to Bob, Reese had another, bigger, claim to fame. He played second base for the Yankees in 1930–1931 and was, for a short time, the one and only baseball roommate the great Babe Ruth ever had as they traveled on road games. People joked that he actually roomed with Babe Ruth's suitcase, as Ruth was known to enjoy the nightlife and didn't spend too much time in his hotel room.

Jimmie Reese, Fungo King, and Babe Ruth's onetime and only roommate. (Source: Fred Jewell/AP/Shutterstock)

"For some reason Jimmie took me under his wing, and we started eating lunch together every now and then. We'd have lunch often at a bakery just south of the ballpark. Jimmie always had the same sandwich, every single time. And every single time, he'd have a ton of stories about the old timers in the game."

When the Tulsa Oilers, a AAA rival team, visited Seattle, they were managed by Warren Spahn, a retired player who has still won more games than any other left-handed pitcher in the history of the game: 363 wins. "Jimmie and Warren were old friends, and Jimmie invited me into the clubhouse. No sandwich this time. I was astounded to be sitting there with Jimmie, Babe Ruth's only roommate, and Warren Spahn, a Hall of Famer with the most wins by a left-handed pitcher in major league history. We were drinking beer and listening to stories about the old timers. And me, I couldn't even make my high school baseball team and hadn't yet seen a major league game live! Amazing."

When Spahn left, he gave a personally signed baseball to Bob. The year was 1967. Bob still has the ball over fifty years later in a pretty nice collection. It's not DNA certified like all the new autographs are, but take it from Certified Bob, it's real.

Pacific Coast League baseball owned by "Certified Bob" and signed by Hall of Fame pitcher Warren Spahn in 1967. (Courtesy of Bob Schoenbachler)

7

Welcome to the Big Leagues

For the remainder of 1967, Bob continued at Peterson Business School during the evenings, while also learning on the job with the AAA Seattle Angels; mostly, the business school time was when the team was on the road and out of town.

Both the AAA Angels staff and the business school faculty were accommodating, especially the faculty who received autographed baseballs as a thank-you from Bob. That also included the night receptionist at the school, "a very good-looking young lady" whom he decided needed a full team–signed ball for being a constant and supportive presence as Bob attended classes at night.

Bob knew things were going well with Katie Schmidt when she asked if his signature was on the ball with all the others. When he responded with a no, she handed it back and asked him to sign it. Within a year, they were married.

"Chuck Tanner was our manager in that 1967 season, and he, too, had a constant smile on his face off the field. Chuck and Jimmie Reese both met Katie later in the year, and both predicted Katie and I would marry. Turns out they were right.

Chuck also kept telling me, 'When you get to the big leagues, you're going to love it.' At the time, that wasn't even an idea anywhere in my head. I kind of just laughed it off."

Meanwhile, Jimmie Reese, Babe Ruth's only roommate, fungo batting expert, and he of the "same sandwich for lunch every time," was instrumental in the next step of Bob's unforeseen transition into the upper echelons of the game.

Bob was about to finally see his first major league game as the Seattle Angels' minor league season came to an end in September 1967. Typically, the minors finished earlier than the majors, allowing for some of the more promising prospects to spend a few weeks at the major league level while those teams were still playing.

Jimmie invited Bob to come to Anaheim to meet Frank Leary, treasurer of the California Angels major league team, to whom Bob had been sending his financial reports. Seattle's team in 1967 was still the AAA affiliate of the Angels and had financial obligations to its parent team.

Bob, of course, was thrilled to take the trip and sit in on important meetings as a twenty-year-old, wet-behind-the-ears auditor who still didn't have his accounting degree.

"Jimmie picked me up at the airport and we went straight to the ballpark. We took a complete tour of the park including the player clubhouses, and then prior to the game we went to the office to meet Frank Leary.

"As we walked into the office, I was floored to see the Angels' owner, Gene Autry, in the room. Next to him stood Roy Disney, brother of famous Walt of Disneyland fame, who looked much like his brother who had passed away the year before. Both Gene and Roy were iconic giants in American entertainment history. Jimmie introduced me to both, and I'm sure they could see how in awe I was in the moment, meeting the world's most famous singing cowboy and meeting the brother of the visionary behind the hugely successful Disneyland franchise that by that time had captured the attention of most of the world."

Autry was far more than a baseball team owner and a singing cowboy, it turns out. To this day, he is the only person to be awarded stars in all five categories on the Hollywood Walk of Fame for film, television, music, radio, and live performance.[1] He was a hugely influential entertainer and is widely credited with bringing country music to a broad national audience.[2]

For decades, Autry also held the record for the bestselling recorded single of all time, "Rudolph the Red-nosed Reindeer," which vied with Bing Crosby's "White Christmas" for the top spot on the list of the country's favorite holiday songs. It sold two million copies on first release (remember, this was 1949–1950), was the first number-one hit of the 1950s, and sold over twenty-five million copies over the next forty years. At one time, Autry was listed as one of the four hundred richest men in the world and was the only entertainer on the list. He's also famous for saying he was better with numbers than he was as an entertainer. In fact, he was a certified public accountant; he also held a private airplane pilot license, and was known as one of the most generous entertainers in the business, giving $180 million to charity.[3]

Bob's next contact with Autry, which occurred early in the season in Seattle, was not quite as awe inspiring for Schoenbachler. It confirmed his suspicion that Autry had more than his share to drink quite often and was likely a severe alcoholic . . . and not necessarily a well-functioning one. "When I was in Autry's presence later, he was so drunk it was unbelievable; he could hardly stand."

Left: Gene Autry getting his horse Champion a drink at the bar of the famous Savoy Hotel in London during his cowboy Hollywood heyday, 1953. (Source: Keystone Press/Alamy Stock Photo) Right: Autry as owner of the California Angels, from whom the Sorianos purchased the AAA franchise that was to become the Pilots . . . and from whom they (unfortunately) hired their first general manager, Marvin Milkes. (Source: Michael Kitada/Orange County Register via ZUMA Wire)

It wasn't clear to Bob how much, if anything, Autry really had to do with day-to-day operations of the franchise at that point. But if he had anything at all to do with those operations, one could easily surmise why they might be having problems.

Autry's trouble with alcohol was described by others, as well: "Gene tells us in his 1978 autobiography that he took control of his drinking. He did not say that he stopped necessarily, but he took control of it, which is how he conducted his life. His stellar successes in the 37 years of his second career tell us that he must have succeeded. No one could sustain that degree of success for so long as a practicing severe alcoholic . . . Facts are facts, as we know, and the facts include that Gene Autry had a demon and a dark side. The demon was alcohol."[4]

On the other hand, Autry did not have a drink named after him, as Dewey Soriano, shortly to become a key leader in Major League Baseball in Seattle, affectionately did. The drink was called Dewey on the Rocks.

"Thinking back, I sometimes think Dewey just wanted to be a shipping pilot, despite his love for baseball. I remember as things with the Pilots team were looking bad and complicated, he used to take out his marine maps and reminisce about his work on the water," Bob recalled.

The drink named after Dewey wasn't associated with Soriano drinking—he didn't drink—but with his history on the waters of Puget Sound. Soriano, it seems, in his earlier career as a ship pilot on the Sound, hit submerged rocks twice, and later, he hit the Duwamish River Bridge (now known as the First Avenue South Bridge). Several Seattle nightspots that attracted customers who spent work time on the water served Dewey on the Rocks with good humor.

"Dewey was lucky his younger brother Max was a good lawyer," according to Bob.

"I eventually met the Angels' treasurer Frank Leary shortly after being stunned into silence in the presence of Autry and Disney; we had a long talk about accounting issues in the major leagues. That night, I saw my first live major league game. After the game, Jimmie took me to a live dinner show with Edie Adams. Jimmie knew a lot of Hollywood stars, and we were supposed to meet Edie Adams after the show, but she was ill and didn't perform. But I got to see her fill-in that night, the great entertainer Jimmy Durante, who had successfully transitioned all the way from vaudeville to his own television show and the movies. Two of Durante's most famous songs, 'As Time Goes By' and 'Make Someone Happy,' were later in the hit movie *Sleepless in Seattle*, an ironic connection. After that trip was when I really started to fantasize a little about a major league role, maybe even replacing Frank Leary as treasurer in California when he retired."

8

Show Me the Money, Seattle

The Sorianos, who had been maneuvering for some time to establish a Seattle major league franchise, officially won the right to field a team at the winter meetings in Mexico City in December 1967. They were awarded the franchise with the understanding that a new stadium would accompany the team before or shortly after its arrival. In initial conversations, that time had been targeted for the early 1970s, at least three and maybe four years out. The dates being thrown around for the major league transition were originally 1971–1972. In early negotiations, the Sorianos considered this a comfortable, affordable, and eminently doable three- or four-year transition period, giving them time to develop more widespread local support. This was initially an understandable and defensible expectation, given their excellent stewardship of the Seattle AAA franchise over many years, and Dewey Soriano's previous status as president of the Pacific Coast League.

Dewey Soriano (left, against the wall), Max Soriano, and Bill Daley (right) in 1967 after being awarded a major league franchise for Seattle; in the moment, it was thought to be the fruition of a dream, but it quickly devolved into an unanticipated nightmare. (Source: David Eskenazi Collection)

Prior to the 1968 transition season opening, the Soriano brothers, Dewey and Max, completed the purchase of the AAA Seattle Angels from California for $75,000, a very high price relative to other minor league purchases at the time. They knew the price was high, but they needed and wanted the team.[1] The sale was facilitated quickly, but no one was doing them any big favors. It was a sign of things to come.

Along with the purchase of the franchise, Seattle decided to hire Marvin Milkes, former assistant general manager of the California Angels. One of his duties for California had been to oversee the Seattle AAA franchise; Milkes was also with California in their start-up as one of the American League's first expansion clubs. On paper, it all looked like obviously helpful experience.

Seattle entered into an independent working agreement for the 1968 season with California as the Angels AAA team. The intent of being independent, of course, was to begin the process of staffing up and "learning all the ropes" in preparation for a major league stadium and transitioning to a major league team. Seattle had a long and storied history of high attendance as a great minor league city, which, they thought, could carry them as they developed other local investors for the major league team.

But things at the major league level were to rapidly change as negotiations with the Sorianos were concluding. The Sorianos, already deeply committed to bringing a major league team to Seattle, had no way out other than to give up the dream. That, they couldn't bring themselves to do.

Alas, the ramp-up timeline and an already paper-thin Soriano pocketbook were blown up by Charlie O. Finley. Finley, who owned the Kansas City franchise, essentially forced the league to expand several years earlier than anticipated to accommodate the demands of Kansas City, which Finley left in the lurch in a move to Oakland for the 1968 season. Kansas City, abandoned by Finley, obtained a promise from MLB to acquire an expansion franchise in 1969. MLB needed another team to balance the schedules.

Meanwhile, Schoenbachler found himself keeping company with Bill Sears, the Seattle team's public relations and promotions guy, handing out information. They were persuading citizens to support a ballot initiative dubbed Forward Thrust, which would support construction of a new stadium among a host of other regional projects. Everyone knew that Seattle's existing Sick's Stadium was not major league level. If Forward Thrust didn't pass, it would likely be a very short stay in Seattle for any major league team. A new stadium was part of the understanding when MLB made the deal with the Sorianos.

Bob recalls, "At this point I really hadn't had much contact with Dewey Soriano, who was president of the Pacific Coast League when the Sorianos bid for the Seattle franchise. You could tell he was confident. A big man physically, he had a presence when he entered the room, the people who knew him would greet him immediately, and he'd be the center of attention. He was pleasant to talk to, and you never felt like he thought he was above you. You were one of the team with Dewey."

Max, with a law degree, was secretary-treasurer of the new Pacific Northwest Sports, Inc., which had been organized to seek the new major league franchise for Seattle.

Despite their prominence in the baseball world, however, the Sorianos were not part of the Seattle high-end monied society or rich corporate world. They were considered on the periphery of the wealthy mainstream. They desperately needed time to grow financial support among these groups, time it appeared they would no longer have.

The two brothers had become the driving force behind Major League Baseball in Seattle, including having a large hand in the proposed Forward Thrust levy. Dewey Soriano had enough baseball influence to have Mickey Mantle, who retired after the 1968 season, come to Seattle prior to the vote to help stump for the passage of Forward Thrust. Other famous players were also enlisted.

Ominously, as they were making the case with MLB for owning the new team, now on a much more aggressive 1969 opening schedule to accommodate the new Kansas City addition and the move by Finley to Oakland, the Sorianos didn't have all the cash to pay the MLB franchise fee up front. No deep-pocketed local partnerships had yet developed, consistent with the fact that they weren't that well-connected to local monied interests. How MLB managed to overlook that rather obvious shortcoming is anyone's guess, but at that point it needed a new team in Seattle as much as the Sorianos wanted one.

To obtain the needed funds to purchase the franchise, Dewey and Max took in an out-of-state partner with deeper pockets, Bill Daley, former owner of the Cleveland Indians and chairman of the Otis Elevator Corporation. At one point, Daley had Seattle on his radar as a destination for his own team, but that idea had not been successful.[2] Daley bought 47 percent of the local franchise, fronting the "bring Major League Baseball to Seattle" effort—Pacific Northwest Sports, Inc., owned by the Sorianos. Together, the Sorianos and Daley put up $1 million in cash, $100,000 of which went to pay the franchise fee for what would become the Pilots.

Because Bob worked the financial numbers, he knew the Sorianos also borrowed $4 million from the Bank of California and borrowed an additional $2 million from the organization that provided concessions throughout major league baseball at the time, Sportservice Corporation. Bob was disappointed to learn only 20 percent of concession profits would go to the team as part of that deal.

Hanging by such a precarious financial thread from the beginning, it was clear that things had to go right very quickly if this risky venture was to succeed.

Meanwhile, adding another few pounds to the financial load, MLB, in its "wisdom," would not be sharing television revenue with the new Pilots for their first three seasons. This left the new Pilots without a portion of the funds being shared by far more established and financially sound teams in the league. If one didn't know better, you'd think the Pilots were being set up to fail.

As things were stacking up, the Pilots appeared more and more behind the eight ball, in an increasingly tough position to be successful.

And finally, the local radio rights were sold in advance of the opening season for far less than hoped. The contract was not terrible, but for a team with few revenue sources, it wasn't nearly what they needed.

Under the above circumstances, even a several-year ramp up would have proven difficult enough. It forced the new franchise into doing some things for which they weren't exactly prepared. An early example was renting out the spring training stadium in Tempe for a rock concert with Janis Joplin to bring in some needed cash. But the stadium was in disrepair and the staff wasn't prepared for the crowd, which knocked down the flimsy outfield walls to get into the concert.

Meanwhile, as part of the 1968 AAA to 1969 major league transition, the AAA team had hired other staff, including a more experienced comptroller late in 1968, nearly the end of the season. Bob now reported to one Phil Duffy.

The anticipated major league front office was beginning to take shape.

Jim Kittilsby, whom Bob met on that first workday of January, had been one of the administrative hires, lifted from the San Francisco Giants.

The entire month of January 1968 was filled with multiple efforts on the part of nearly everyone associated with the Seattle team to make sure the Forward Thrust levy passed. All of the Soriano eggs were in the levy basket. Fortunately for all concerned, the levy passed in February. It was welcome good news that energized the Sorianos and the staff and provided a new stadium at public expense, albeit some years later than desired given the accelerated MLB schedule.

While Bob and Jim and many other staff were having a good time in the excitement of the year-long ramp up, unfortunately, Bob and new boss Phil Duffy did not have a mutually pleasant relationship.

Bob knew he was in for a rough ride from the beginning. "Phil Duffy walked in at season's end as a new hire and immediately informed me in no uncertain terms that I would be his 'assistant' and he was the boss. My first thought was 'Wow, what an insecure guy.'"

Duffy, for instance, got a kick out of taking Bob to lunch at a still-existing iconic restaurant called 13 Coins, intentionally ordering a Caesar salad with anchovies for Bob, and watching Bob squirm while he ate it. "I ate it just to save face," Bob recalls. "I almost got sick right then and there. Duffy took pleasure in being the one with power."

"Our offices were outside Sick's Stadium in trailers," Bob recalls, "and the first thing Duffy did was put up a false wall between him and my cubicle, to form his own private office. He spent most of his time in there with his feet on the desk, talking on the phone to nobody in particular. He hardly did a thing with the auditing paperwork, except to let me do all the detail, which I liked, then he took my reports to ownership. I think they were quickly catching up with his act. They didn't like his arrogance or his work ethic, which wasn't much at the time. Duffy was a bow-down-to-God guy, and he thought he was God."

As the 1968 season came to an end in September, Bob went to owner Dewey Soriano and asked if he could continue as auditor of the minor league team at least through December, the end of the year, since who would be included in the future transition from a AAA team to a major league team was still murky. "Dewey gladly and easily granted my request. I was somewhat relieved they granted my request so quickly."

After 1968, Bob was unsure of what might be next for him in baseball or anywhere else, for that matter.

Shortly after the 1968 season ended, the team entered into the October draft of players from other major league teams to fill the roster of the new 1969 Seattle major league team . . .

a transition much earlier than anticipated due to the Kansas City-to-Oakland fiasco. Bob added a player to his team, too, marrying Katie Schmidt on October 19, 1968, after the season concluded and just after the expansion draft.

In November 1968, Bob was called into Dewey Soriano's office, just a month before Bob was prepared to end his stint with the AAA Seattle club. Sitting on the couch in Soriano's office, Bob was startled with another revelation and unexpected transition.

"We would like you to know we fired Phil Duffy today and we want you to take his place with the new major league team."

It was a totally unexpected (and undiscussed) invitation. It turns out Duffy's time supposedly "setting up and then overseeing the financial health and obligations" with the new team was far shorter than the history of the Pilots a year later. One of the Sorianos' first major hires struck out after a quick at-bat, and took an intentional walk out the door after only four months on the job.

9

A Too-Early Team with Too Many Errors

Seattle's new major league franchise was largely on its way, thanks in part to the success of the Forward Thrust levy, which included money for a new stadium and was championed aggressively by the Sorianos. However, an accelerated timeline forced the Sorianos and the city to plan for the arrival of its new team in 1969, rather than the original timeline of 1971–1972. A new stadium was years away. In the meantime, old and deteriorating Sick's Stadium would have to suffice.

Unconcerned with Seattle, Charlie O. Finley, owner of the Kansas City franchise, had made an independent decision to leave Kansas City in winter 1967. Kansas City had become the butt of many jokes, including being the "minor league AAA team for the Yankees." New York had pulled off several trades with Kansas City, nearly always to the detriment of Kansas City. That included the trade to New York of one Roger Maris, who in 1961 would break Babe Ruth's long-standing single season home run record of sixty. Maris would hit sixty-one in a close home run race with teammate Mickey Mantle.

Finley swore he would leave Kansas City and start the 1968 season in Oakland, come hell or high water. Some have suggested that both hell and high water arrived soon after his pledge. Other major league owners were not happy. They resisted, but finally relented on October 18, 1967, giving "permission" for Finley to move to Oakland. Finley might have moved to Oakland anyway, but when the other owners saw a prolonged fight ahead, they relented.

Charlie Finley (center), whose controversial move of his team from Kansas City to Oakland fatefully accelerated the start-up timeline of the Seattle Pilots. (Source: National Baseball Library/Doug McWilliams)

At the time, the Sorianos and MLB had already agreed in principle to provide an MLB franchise to Seattle but based on a different timeline. While the contract was yet to be officially awarded, the Sorianos had already begun searching for administrative talent, including a call to Jim Kittilsby that October.

In response to Finley's moving of their team to Oakland, Kansas City immediately sued Major League Baseball, demanding a team be put back in Kansas City. The city had made several previous financial commitments over the years to the team. In return, Kansas City had received, in its view, an implied promise to retain the team in the city.

Between a rock and a hard place, Major League Baseball promised to give Kansas City a new team "in a few years" and suggested the addition could come at the same time Seattle was to be "added" to the league to ensure balanced scheduling. The intended date was 1971–1972, consistent with the timeline of adding a Seattle team.

Kansas City gave that idea an adamant, loud "No!"

The no was so loud it was heard in the halls of Congress in Washington, DC. Missouri's powerful senator, Stuart Symington, threatened to go to Congress and remove the antitrust shield that protected MLB unlike almost any other corporate institution in America. Such protection allowed them to limit the number of franchises and maintain a monopoly on the game. It also helped them eliminate competition for players, enabling them to more tightly control salaries.

In fact, the antitrust shield was a major element in making the purchase and sale of baseball teams such a lucrative venture for the already very wealthy. The idea of losing that shield panicked the owners.

Baseball Commissioner Bowie Kuhn relented under the legal and political pressure. He promised a franchise to Kansas City within a year, in 1969. The pressure from the congressman disappeared, much to the relief of the major league hierarchy.

To balance the now new Kansas City team schedule with that of another team, Seattle's MLB timeline was hastily moved up to 1969, just after the Sorianos had purchased the AAA Angels to begin their preparation and enhance the learning curve of new staff.

This acceleration also meant Seattle would have to play its early years in old and deteriorating Sick's Stadium. Even if a new stadium was approved, it would take multiple years to finish.

Whether this decision to accelerate and play in a stadium clearly needing huge upgrades constituted strike one, two, or three can be debated, but it was definitely a call not in Seattle's favor. In fact, almost every call being made was not in Seattle's favor.

A new stadium in Seattle was years away. Financing for the franchise was still being lined up, and deep pockets weren't all that anxious to jump in. The economic boom appeared to be slowing. In addition, the proposed Boeing SST program showed signs of trouble (in fact, the program was canceled in 1970, resulting in a 50 percent cut in Boeing employment in the region and the now-famous billboard stating "Will the last person leaving SEATTLE - turn out the lights").

And thus began both the beginning, and the end, of the Seattle Pilots.

Pacific Northwest Sports, Inc., headed by the Sorianos, was granted a major league franchise in December 1967. But now, play was to begin in 1969, much earlier than anticipated, and the Sorianos and MLB were too committed to back out. With this accelerated timeline, the group was far from being prepared and adequately financed.

"There were not proper offices, equipment was old and inadequate, there were no adding machines even. Everything was done by hand. The stadium was deteriorated. It was a fingers-in-the-dike operation from the beginning. Mass confusion and rush, rush, rush," remembers Schoenbachler. "Completely disorganized, few systems in place, everything accelerated," affirmed Jim Kittilsby.

But there were other factors contributing to the impending disaster, many of them having to do with leadership, or lack of it, in key management positions.

The Sorianos' first and most important administrative hire for the 1968–1969 transition year proved to be a major mistake. Marvin Milkes was hired away from the California Angels to fill the position of general manager of the AAA Seattle Angels in 1968 to the Seattle Pilots in 1969 and beyond. It made sense on paper, as Milkes's job with the California major league team included oversight of the AAA Seattle Angels. The highly popular Edo Vanni was shuffled from GM back into the administrative structure and given the title Director of Group Sales.

Milkes would begin immediately in 1968, serving as the general manager of the independent AAA team owned by the Sorianos as part of the transition, and would be responsible for preparing for the expansion draft of players from other teams in the fall of 1968.

Bob, meanwhile, was offered the job of comptroller of the new Seattle major league team at the end of that same 1968 season after the dramatically quick Duffy failure. The offer to Bob was made three times. Thrilled to be asked, he nevertheless turned it down twice. "I don't want that job. It's over my head," he told them. Having Duffy for his "mentor" hadn't been much help. Indeed, it hadn't been any help at all.

But the Sorianos persisted. "Look, we've done our due diligence. We've checked with Dick Pahre at Price Waterhouse, who audit our books annually. They indicate you've done a fine job straightening things out with our AAA team. They told us we have somebody well qualified right here in-house, and that somebody is you." And obviously, they'd seen Bob dig deep into many facets of the organization on the administrative side, seeking to know and understand how each area impacted the books.

Bob relented in November 1968 on their third appeal, enticed by a $1,000 a month offer, basically doubling his salary in one fell swoop.

With the transition early in 1969 into the Seattle Pilots, Bob would become the youngest comptroller in the history of Major League Baseball at age twenty-one, a record that still stands over fifty years later and is quite likely to last forever, given the financial complexity of today's game.

Bob Schoenbachler, circa 1967, the year he was hired by the Seattle Angels. In roughly twenty-four months, he rose from being an unemployed student scanning a business school placement board to chief financial officer of a major league baseball team. (Source: Bob Schoenbachler)

Bob recalled having a smile on his face after learning about the huge salary increase. "I was in Shit Heaven." He was also newly married, of course, having taken the plunge immediately after the October draft of the new team. "It was quite the wedding present."

Had the Sorianos done the same level of due diligence with Marvin Milkes, their general manager, as they later did with Bob, they might have had a fighting chance. A slim chance, perhaps, even with the unexpected early arrival of Major League Baseball in Seattle, a deteriorating stadium, no committed local deep pockets, no television profit sharing, and only 20 percent of concession profits. But they didn't do the deeper dive into Milkes's background.

"He was one of the most paranoid guys I ever met," recalls Bob, witness to it all. "He wasn't a bad baseball man, knowing the players, but the trouble was he was an idiot in many other ways, and really weird. He had a terrible temper, kicked holes in his desk, couldn't handle disagreement, and just went his own way despite attempts to help him be better informed. He was unglued half the time, and weird the other half. In the end, rather than put up with his bullshit, people would just avoid him or not tell him the truth. People were intimidated into being yes-men, or nowhere to be found." Jim Kittilsby agreed, noting, "I got along with him fine, but many others were not so lucky."

The California Angels, undoubtedly, had seen some of this dysfunction when Milkes was their vice president and assistant general manager. They forgot to mention it to the Sorianos, apparently, and the Sorianos apparently didn't ask the right questions in this case. On paper, Milkes's qualifications looked good. The reality was turning out to be quite different.

"The only person to end up on the right side of that deal was a member of our grounds crew," Bob remembers. "For some reason Milkes took a liking to him, and he benefited from one of Milkes's quirks, which was that he never wore a shirt more than one time. So, each day, Milkes would wear a shirt, then send clubhouse man Fred Genzale to a clothier to buy a new one for the next day and give the grounds-crew guy his 'old' shirt. I'm sure the grounds-crew guy was the best-dressed grounds-crew member in all of baseball. I think all clubhouse man Genzale got was about seventy-five boring trips to the clothing store and back."

Bob remembers, "I avoided Milkes like the plague, as did most everyone else. I just went straight to the Sorianos for anything I needed, because by this time I was establishing a good relationship with them."

It was just as well. Partly because nobody would argue with Milkes or tell him things he didn't want to hear, it was widely conceded that Kansas City, the other new franchise, outdrafted Seattle in the October 1968 expansion draft of players for the 1969 team. That the Pilots had philosophically decided to "draft mainly older players people had heard of" in order to help boost attendance might also have had something to do with it. Again, their undercapitalized start, combined with a poor deal from MLB, almost forced such a move since so much of the book balancing would be dependent upon attendance.

Another nail in the coffin of the short-lived franchise.

Nobody knows for sure, but another reason Seattle was outdrafted, Bob speculates, was that "Milkes left his briefcase in a taxicab with his entire draft list in it, along with some of the financials related to the team. The items were never recovered. That happened on the way home after the draft, but if he was that loose with such critical information, identifying which players he valued most and which he didn't, who knows what else happened earlier or later as trades were proposed?"

To make a bad draft class even worse, Milkes managed to trade away the Pilots' best player of the draft, Lou Piniella. Piniella was the Pilots' fourteenth pick in the expansion draft, from Cleveland. After the trade, Piniella became Rookie of the Year in the American League. Ironically, he was traded to, played for, and won the Rookie of the Year award with the new team in Kansas City, of all places.

The Piniella trade was completed on April Fools' Day 1969, just a few days before the season began. It ended up being only slightly less foolish than the trick the team would play on April Fools' Day 1970 as they ended spring training.

In any event, one can legitimately wonder if some of that loose draft information had anything to do with the Kansas City decision to target Piniella in a trade, knowing, perhaps, he wasn't highly valued in Seattle. Speculation, of course. But the trade did happen after the draft information disappeared.

Dick Bates, Lou's roommate during spring training with Seattle, confirmed, though, that Lou and his field manager, Joe Schultz, did not see eye to eye. Lou was the epitome of a classic hard driver. Schultz was just the opposite. "I remember Lou was having to run a lot of laps in the outfield all the time as a form of punishment from Schultz, usually because Lou never hesitated to express his opinion."

Schultz was popular with most players, but Piniella was known for his fiercely competitive manner, and Schultz's laid-back approach might have been a source of some of Piniella's angst. He was happy to be selected by an expansion team, as he had contemplated quitting baseball after seven years in the minor leagues with three different organizations and not much of a look in the majors. If it wasn't for the Pilots picking him in the expansion draft, he could have retired a journeyman minor leaguer at the end of 1968.[1] But having been selected by Seattle, the intense Piniella was apparently not a good fit. Jim Bouton in *Ball Four* noticed:

> Piniella is a case. He hits the hell out of the ball. He hit a three-run homer today and he's got

a .400 average, but they're easing him out. He complains a lot about the coaches and ignores them when he feels like it, and to top it off he's sensitive as hell to things like Joe Schultz not saying good morning to him. None of this is supposed to count when you judge a ballplayer's talents. But it does.[2]

This excerpt from Bruce Markusen's August 24, 2014, blog entry from VintageDetroit.com might help to clarify the gap between Piniella's competitive streak and Schultz's laid-back approach:

> Although Schultz played major league ball as a catcher in the late 1930s and 1940s, he did not really enter the public spotlight until the 1968 World Series between the Tigers and the Cardinals.
>
> As NBC cameras showed him coaching third base for the National League champion Cardinals, broadcasters Curt Gowdy and Harry Caray repeatedly referred to him as the first manager in the history of the [new 1969] Seattle Pilots. The announcers talked so much about Schultz that he became one of the subplots to the Series.
>
> Mind you, Pilots general manager Marvin Milkes refused to make the news of Schultz' hiring official until the ninth inning of Game Seven, but it was baseball's worst kept secret that the expansion Pilots had already chosen him as their inaugural manager for 1969.
>
> At the time of Schultz' rumored hiring, he was virtually unknown outside of St. Louis. As

a result of being relatively unknown, in January and February of 1969, Schultz made the rounds in the Great Northwest. He attended everything from lunch-time school programs to business luncheons to evening banquets and Sunday church socials. With his good nature and wisecracking sense of humor, Schultz became a hit on the wintertime circuit. He told anyone who would listen that the Pilots could finish third in the American League West. Given his energy, enthusiasm and sincerity, most fans seemed to believe him.

Schultz became even better known after the release of *Ball Four*, Jim Bouton's groundbreaking diary of his 1969 baseball season, which Bouton split between the Pilots and the Astros. Schultz emerged as one of the overriding characters in the book. According to Bouton, Schultz delivered unique motivational speeches to his players, talks that were filled with humor, clichés, and plenty of profanity.

On one occasion, as related by Bouton, Schultz lauded his Pilots for blowing out the opposition. "Attaway to stomp 'em," Schultz exhorted his troops. "Stomp the piss out of 'em. Stomp 'em when they're down. Kick 'em and stomp 'em."

One of Schultz' most memorable exchanges took place during a visit to the mound with pitcher John Gelnar, as described by Bouton in this excerpt:

Gelnar was telling us about this great conversation he had with Joe on the mound. There were a couple of guys on and [the Tigers] Tom

Matchick was up. "Any particular way you want me to pitch him, Joe?" Gelnar asked.

"Nah, bleep him," Joe Schultz said. "Give him some low smoke and we'll go and pound some Budweiser."

Those last three words became Schultz' infamous catch phrase. He enjoyed telling his players to finish off the game and pick up a win so that they could all "pound some Budweiser."

Unfortunately, the Pilots pounded Budweiser mostly after losses. They didn't have the talent to finish third, as Schultz had once hoped.[3]

As time progressed, Jim Bouton was coming home from each road trip loaded with pages of handwritten notes, which he'd ask whomever was handy to copy for him. *Ball Four* was in the works, about to make Schultz even more famous than during his World Series "reveal."

"Schultz was friendly but not blessed with social grace," Jim Kittilsby noted with some affection. "I remember him growing antsy at a player-personnel staff meeting, finally exiting by saying aloud to no one in particular, 'I've got to go drop a load of mud.'" Shocked silence was followed by smiles, chuckles, shaking heads, and eye rolls as Schultz left the room, supposedly headed for the bathroom.

Lou Piniella, meanwhile, known for his intense competitiveness and no-nonsense fire, was long gone to Kansas City, and as his career progressed, that intensity became more and more obvious. He later won two World Series titles as a player with the New York Yankees and, ironically, also made a triumphant return to Seattle, becoming the intense, masterful, and occasionally infamous manager of the Seattle Mariners. He was so mad after one Seattle game that he overturned the food table, and the Sterno heating the food trays set the clubhouse carpet on fire. Pitcher Chris Bosio was said to have stopped the fire with a carton of milk, which smelled up the clubhouse for days after.[4] Piniella managed the Mariners through their greatest years to date, from 1993 to 2002.

Left: Lou Piniella as a Pilot before his trade to Kansas City prior to opening day on April Fools' Day 1969. (Source: Charles Kapner Collection) Right: Lou showing off his kicking style during a tantrum as intense manager of the Seattle Mariners many years later. (Source: Elaine Thompson/AP/Shutterstock)

General Manager Milkes was said to have disliked Piniella, and it was he who traded him away. Bill Schonely, radio announcer for the team, has been quoted as saying, "The players hated Milkes; everyone was upset over that trade."[5] Jim Bouton in *Ball Four* confirmed this view, shrewdly observing, "Marvin Milkes is not a guy who will sit around in a situation that calls for panic."[6]

Milkes managed to last the first and only year of the Seattle Pilots franchise, then moved to Milwaukee with the team after the Seattle Pilots declared bankruptcy.

The new Milwaukee owners had little choice but to keep Milkes the first year in Milwaukee, as the decision to allow the move to Milwaukee from Seattle came so near the start of the season (six days). Specifically, it came on the last day of spring training, in April 1970. But by December 1970, Milkes was gone despite having signed an extension with Bud Selig. Keeping Milkes in the Seattle-to-Milwaukee transition was "the biggest baseball mistake I ever made," Selig later told Bob.

Having missed on Milkes as did Bud Selig a year later, the snake-bit Sorianos had to scramble in other ways in their ill-fated attempt to permanently bring Major League Baseball to Seattle. Milkes, unfortunately, was far from their only mistake.

Dewey and Max had already missed on their original hire for an intended major league finance guy with Duffy, but with Certified Bob in place, in whom they had great trust, they were saved from greater embarrassment. Misses on several other hires, as we shall see, would become apparent.

On another front, the Sorianos knew Sick's Stadium wasn't up to par, and a new stadium was years away. During spring training in Phoenix in early 1968, the so-called transition year in which they owned the AAA Angels independently, they were working with some contractors who had helped build the spring training site, Diablo Stadium in Tempe. Bob was there on the Sorianos' behalf, having taken his first business trip ever. He was to review the contractors' books "to see where all the money went."

"Because they were in such a hurry to get the stadium presentable, and because they were undercapitalized, I think the Sorianos got wrapped up with some people they never should have got wrapped up with. To me it seemed that there were crooks on the left and crooks on the right in the contracting businesses with whom they were having conversations. The contractors kept letting me know they were 'very good friends' with 'Joe,' and I had no idea who he was or why they kept bringing him up. They would mention 'Joe' again and I'd think in my head, 'Who the hell is Joe?' I found out later they were talking about Joe Bananas [Bonnano], mafia boss, who had a home in Tucson."

After those Phoenix meetings regarding construction on the spring training site, Bob recalls thinking, "There seemed to be some weird expenses, but I was twenty-one or twenty-two years old and getting ready for the season. I reported this at first to the Sorianos. Nothing ever came of it, so I just kept my mouth shut after that."

Jim Kittilsby also spent time in Phoenix during that 1968 transition year and ran the fall instructional league for minor league players. Earlier that year, his first spring training orders were indicative of the questionable level of sophistication in the transition year. Said Dewey Soriano, "You know baseball . . . go make sure stadium locker rooms don't look like high school, and make sure the pitcher's mound is right."

Knowing many of the players at this point, Jim was also helping retain and protect players Seattle didn't want to lose to the ongoing war in Vietnam. He became an expert in enrolling players in certain colleges to keep the players out of the draft or getting them into the National Guard or Reserves. As others in the league got wind of this particular strategy, Jim became the pipeline to college entry for other players on other teams. Having already worked for several franchises, Jim had a growing list of contacts throughout the league.

Ready or not, after working their way through the transition year of 1968 and now 1969 spring training, the first and only shaky season of the Pilots began.

The new Seattle Pilots entered the 1969 season, made famous by Jim Bouton in *Ball Four*, with a seemingly unstable general manager with whom no one would converse unless forced; a twenty-one-year-old comptroller just out of business school who didn't want the job because he thought it was over his head; an old stadium falling apart at the seams; an undercapitalized and scrambling ownership with a much shorter transition time than anticipated; a major owner and partner who didn't live anywhere near the Northwest; little forthcoming financial support yet developed in the community; several team administrative hires that didn't go through much of a vetting process and whose job performances were quickly proving to be questionable; and a team drafted from a list that may have been in the hands of its competing Kansas City expansion team for all anyone knew.

In addition, the team uniforms were being modeled by one Jim Kittilsby for publicity photos, as no actual players were available when the uniforms were being developed.

It wasn't what one would call a surefire formula for success, shall we say.

Jim Kittilsby, Pilots administrator, modeling the newly designed Pilots road uniform in 1969. Note the hat design, which was not yet completed and later was changed. (Courtesy of Jim Kittilsby)

It took one day—opening day, April 11, 1969—for Bob and Jim and several others to realize this might be a short-lived franchise.

A reconfigured Sick's Stadium at first had been "promised" by city officials to have thirty thousand seats. The Sorianos were later informed by the city that for multiple safety and sanitation reasons, twenty-five thousand seats would be the maximum available. But even those weren't available—construction was still occurring on opening day.

As luck would have it, the Pilots had not sold out opening day in advance. In fact, season ticket sales had not been nearly as robust as expected. Bob recalls, "There were cases [where] the team got phone calls for bills sent for season tickets, and the caller . . . or I should say numerous callers . . . said, 'I didn't order any season tickets.' It's fair to say something wasn't well-coordinated in the office." That may have been the case, but the fact that Seattle had priced its tickets higher than almost any other team in Major League Baseball was likely also a big factor. They did so, of course, because the deal with MLB was so bad that ticket sales were nearly the only source of revenue able to make projections of success actually appear to work on paper.

Despite low season-ticket sales, the opening day walk-up crowd was large, and additional seats were being installed, literally nailed in and painted, as the crowd arrived. The new seat numbers and locations were being called in to the ticket office by walkie-talkie so that the just-constructed seats could be sold to the walk-up opening-day crowd.

Bill Mullins, who wrote about the Seattle Pilots' opening day in *Becoming Big League*, described it this way:

> Early comers to the home opener heard the banging of carpenters hammering more seats into place. Estimates varied on how many seats were actually available by game time out of the 25,000 promised. Some said there were as few as 16,000; [others] said more than 18,000 but less than 25,000. The most accurate estimate was probably around 19,500. Attendance was 15,014, a low number for the first major league game in Seattle history.[7]

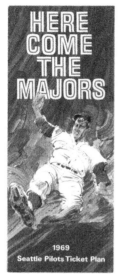 

Left: Pilots Ticket Plan, which was likely printed in late 1968 for early ticket sales. Team colors on the brochure were incorrect. Right: Opening day ticket. (Courtesy of Chris McKinney)

Bob recalls, "It was the city's responsibility to bring the stadium up to standards, as that was a role they agreed to play in helping to bring Major League Baseball to Seattle. But for some reason, the city and their contractor for stadium work never seemed to get their act together and get on the same page at the same time. The end result was an opening day fiasco."

"That day cost us more than it helped us," said Jim Kittilsby. Bob Schoenbachler agreed, recalling, "We received all kinds of dry-cleaning bills from people who had sat on recently painted seats. We paid them all."

In a 1994 interview, Bill Sears confirmed much the same thing, with an added flourish. "We put in wooden bleachers, but the wood was not the best [probably a cost-cutting move]; fans would get splinters. One guy had a brand-new suit and he ripped the seat right out of his pants. We had two or three of those happen."[8]

Sick's Stadium, Seattle, April 10, 1969, on the evening before opening day, with rough bleachers and the scoreboard still being installed. (Source: Newspapers.com)

In contrast to Sick's Stadium in Seattle, this is Municipal Stadium in Kansas City, 1969, where the new Kansas City team opened the season. (Public Domain)

The water pressure was bad, too, so neither the bathrooms nor the water faucets were consistently working when the stadium opened. In fact, low water pressure had been a long-standing problem with the old stadium and had never worked well with big crowds. Ominously, with the city and their contractor faltering, and without the necessary financial power to fix the water system themselves, the Pilots opened the season anyway. Figuratively speaking, things were going down the toilet right from the start . . . just not in the way they were supposed to.

Visiting teams were often forced to take showers in their hotels instead of at the stadium after games because of the poor water pressure. And when attendance was above ten thousand (which didn't happen often, frankly) the toilet in the press box couldn't even be flushed until late in the game. This resulted in what came to be not-so-fondly known by the attending press corps as "the seventh-inning flush."

The rumor is that Bill Sears, the marketing man who tagged Bob Schoenbachler with the "Certified Bob" title and had a good relationship with some of the sports writers, also had a little something to do with the seventh-inning moniker.

To top it all off, so to speak, the outfield bleachers were serviced by what are today commonly called "porta potties," although that was not the company supplying them. Regardless, that's not what you would call major league quality, and in fact it was clearly worse than many minor league stadiums.

One story making the rounds at the time was that a fan got locked in one of those portable toilets all night. According to Bill Sears and confirmed by Bob and Jim, "The janitors came in the morning to clean, opened the door, and out popped this guy. They just about fainted. He probably had a few too many Rainiers [a local popular beer] and fell asleep in the john, then got locked in."

Another opening day snafu was that Cathi Soriano, owner Dewey's twelve-year-old daughter, was taken just outside the stadium before the game to meet a star scheduled to sing the national anthem. Her escort to see the star returned inside the stadium, and Cathi was unable to get back in because she didn't have a ticket. She was outside crying until someone came out and rescued her.[9]

"Basically, opening day was a disaster," Bob recalls. "And while it's widely reported these days that the stadium had twenty-five thousand seats, the truth is we never had more than a little over twenty-four thousand the entire season. I know, because it was my job to know. And we never did fill all of those with the exception of one day, and that was bat day when we only ordered half the bats we needed based on past attendance figures earlier in the season. So that day was a disaster, too.

"Our two largest attendance days left a huge number of fans very disappointed in their experience."

April 11 versus the Chicago White Sox also opened eyes in other ways.

Jim Kittilsby recalls, "On opening day, everyone was scrambling around trying to help, even if they didn't exactly know what to do or how to do it."

Everyone, it turned out, except the director of the Pilots' speakers bureau, Herb Elk, also a Soriano hire. Dewey Soriano was already beginning to have his doubts about Herb not long after he was hired.

Elk was a large guy, so large he had the driver's seat removed from his car and drove from a rearranged seat moved into the back seat area. "Weirdest thing I ever saw," Bob remembers.

Kittilsby added, "Despite being so big, Herb was meek as a mouse, and seemed always afraid of something happening to him. He was so scared he started wearing a shoulder holster under his sport coat, with a weapon in it. You could see it bulging out from his coat all the time. And as head of the speakers bureau, when he made presentations to the public with his coat unbuttoned, his shoulder holster and gun were visible. You have to wonder how people he was talking to responded in terms of deciding to buy tickets and support the team." This was highly out of the ordinary in 1968, and Dewey finally saw it one day. "I remember Dewey asking me incredulously, 'Is he carrying a gun to work?' I had to tell him yes."

Kittilsby continued, "So come opening day, and already being somewhat suspect, this guy was sitting in his office—I'm not embellishing—perusing his rare comic books collection while everyone around him was scrambling to make things work.

"He had this big collection of old comics. He had kind of a fetish about old comic books. The rest of us were just overwhelmed with opening-day stuff—the paint was barely dry. Well, actually, the paint wasn't dry in a number of places. In any event, everyone was doing two or three things at once. Dewey Soriano, the team president, while scurrying past Herb's office, saw Herb sitting there admiring his collection of classic comic books while everyone else was flying around in half panic. Stunned at the sight, Soriano fired him on the spot. This confirmed, obviously, another early and critical hiring mistake of someone in an important and very public position. Two down already, the finance guy and the public relations speakers bureau guy, and we hadn't even completed opening day. And number three was the GM Milkes, whom everyone could already see was going to be trouble," Kittilsby said.

And thus did Jim Kittilsby suddenly also become director of the speakers bureau, in addition to his other tasks. The speakers bureau was no small addition to Jim's growing list of "other responsibilities"; he fulfilled 103 speaking engagements after taking on the role.

Such was life as an administrator with the Seattle Pilots.

As the early season progressed, with all its bumps and bruises and ruined customer suits, the California Angels came to town on April 28 for a short series. It was here that Bob saw Gene Autry, the Angels owner, once again. But this time it was pretty clear that Autry didn't see much of anyone else. Visiting with the Pilots' owner Dewey Soriano, Autry was, as they say, "fish-flopping drunk." To insiders, this was nothing new. Since World War II, Autry had turned more and more to alcohol, and his once-lofty position in the entertainment industry as a radio, television, and recording performer had already deteriorated because of it.

As Bob was reviewing the day's ticket sales after the California game, a man Bob had never seen before entered the office. Taking the unlit cigar from his mouth, he announced in a high-pitched voice, "I'm Tommy Ferguson, and I'm here to pick up a check for our share of today's ticket sales. Frank Leary sent me."

Leary was with the California Angels, the visiting team, who were to receive 20 percent of the gate receipts. Rather obviously, the Angels—and perhaps others in the league—were already concerned about the Pilots' cash flow. Schoenbachler balked. His first test as a rookie comptroller. "Forget it, that's not happening," he responded. "I don't know you. I'll mail in the receipts like I'm supposed to." Ferguson turned and walked out. The rookie passed his first test.

Bob later learned, a bit to his embarrassment, that Ferguson was the traveling secretary of the California Angels. Given Bob's characteristic commitment to protecting team assets, it's unlikely he would have handed Ferguson a check even knowing who he was. The American League operating procedure was to send a check to the visiting team after the home stand, and even though this was a very early Pilots game, Bob was up to speed on proper procedure. Bill Sears didn't pick Bob's nickname of Certified Bob out of a hat. Bob earned it.

Ferguson and Bob would reunite later in the year, as he, too, was hired by the Sorianos.

It turns out Tommy Ferguson started his baseball career as a batboy for the Boston Braves. Over the years he climbed the baseball ladder all the way to vice president and traveling secretary, quite a distance from batboy. After Seattle, he made the transition to Milwaukee, as did Bob and Jim and Bill Sears, among a few others. Said Bob, "Tommy seemed to know everybody in baseball and was very well liked and respected."

Later in Milwaukee, Tommy, who first appeared to Bob as a questionable character hot to get his hands on Seattle's meager cash flow, or at least California's 20 percent of the gate receipts, became best friends with Bob and his wife.

10

Going Nowhere Leads to Going Elsewhere

Troubles continued to mount.

"Our special promotions guy . . . hat day, bat day, and so on . . . it turns out he was a wheeler-dealer and not all that trustworthy," said Bob, adding to a growing list of suspect new hires. "He was hired without much vetting, also from Houston as was Herb Elk, a contact made through one of Dewey's 'friends,' although Bill Sears was reported as saying Marvin Milkes convinced the Sorianos to hire the guy. As a promotions guy, he always seemed to order more stuff than needed, and the excess somehow disappeared."

Bob and Jim recall the guy's loaner Buick being filled with promotional items, which he apparently gave away out of the trunk with abandon. He had "moved to Washington State with his wife and her hairdresser," laughed Jim, lending an air of speculative curiosity to the already eye-rolling environment. His hiring was another unforced error, and Dewey Soriano eventually let him go, too.

Said Bill Sears, "He wasn't doing anything, so Dewey fired him somewhere in the middle of the summer."[1] Four important administrative figures already down . . . and others were under suspicion.

When this latest firing occurred, more was added to Jim Kittilsby's growing list of titles and responsibilities. "There were no systems in place; we were doing everything by the seat of our pants . . . hiring, promotions procurement, stadium repairs, you name it . . . we made it up on the spot as we went along, depending most of the time on relationships or bartering or just plain guessing. It was chaos."

"You could feel the tensions rise as the team floundered, the old park continued to be a problem in almost every way, the team was really bad, and attendance sagged," Bob recalled. "By early June, just sixty days in, I really knew something was up. I think the Sorianos knew it earlier than that, as the lack of talent on the team became obvious and attendance was obviously less than hoped. Max Soriano would be coming in nearly every day asking new questions and wanting to know how attendance was matching up against projections. Obviously, the real attendance wasn't matching up. Then Max started asking me for different, weird kinds of reports. I don't recall all the different reports he wanted, but they were out of the routine and required me to research new stuff and put it in a report."

In an interview years later, Max Soriano confirmed Bob's instinct that the Sorianos knew they were in trouble. Said Max, "I knew early on it was going to be a very, very difficult period, because in early May we had a series with the Boston Red Sox coming to town, I think on a Tuesday evening. It was just a beautiful evening, and I was thinking to myself we're going to really draw the people—because here was Yastrzemski, who had been instrumental in the 1968 bond issue, and Reggie Smith and some of these outstanding ballplayers coming to town . . . and we drew just . . . seven thousand people."[2]

"Things weren't too organized in the ticket office, either," Bob remembers. "There was concern about cash coming in and disappearing. The auditors made a point to say the facilities were not proper for a ticket office. One night an auditor and I went into the ticket office after everyone left to see if we could find anything that would lead us to a culprit, but we just stumbled around in the dark and couldn't find a damn thing."

Stumbling around in the dark was a common theme during that year, it seems. With a minor league team in a more modest transition period, constantly stumbling around in the dark may not have been as large an issue, but with a major league team and the future of that team on the line, it was debilitating.

Meanwhile, the new team in Kansas City was doing just fine, making the comparison embarrassing for the Sorianos and the Seattle franchise.

Of course, looking back, Kansas City had local owners with deeper pockets, an established major league culture, and a well-established team brand. But in the heat of the moment in Seattle, none of that mattered much. All Seattle knew was that the new Pilots were failing, and the new Kansas City team was thriving. And Kansas City was doing it with an exciting young player Seattle had owned just weeks ago, Lou Piniella, who was on his way to claiming the American League Rookie of the Year trophy as a Kansas City player.

"By this time," Bob recalls, "I was updating projections weekly, knowing we had to hit about twelve thousand five hundred fully paid tickets a game. Ticket sales were our lifeblood, our main source of revenue. If we failed to sell tickets, we would be in big trouble. We weren't doing it, not even close. Other clubs were also getting revenue-sharing funds from the MLB Central Fund, but Seattle was not to be included in that resource until 1972. So, I was working commercial paper with our cash, buying and selling on almost a day-trader basis, trying to earn extra cash through arbitrage. Bank of California complained to Max and Dewey, wanting me to stop, because basically we were taking the risk with their loaned dollars. And I remember Dewey calling me into the office.

Bob took a seat at Dewey's insistence.

"Dewey opens the conversation by saying, 'Bank of California is concerned about your investments in overnight commercial paper; they say you are risking the borrowed cash.' I asked Dewey what he wanted me to do. 'Well, so far you are bringing in extra cash, right? Just keep doing what you're doing. That's all.' And that's the end of the meeting. I had to smile to myself as I walked out, knowing Dewey both liked and needed that extra cash.

"Shortly after that meeting, I had a talk with Max Soriano, the lawyer and logical side of the family. I knew he knew, but I said to him, 'Max, we are in need of more capital. If we don't do better soon we may have a problem at the end of the season.'

"Max and Dewey went to Bill Daley, the original investor with forty-seven percent of the company and former owner of the Cleveland Indians. He had previously considered moving the Cleveland team to Seattle several years earlier, so he obviously had some affinity for the area. But Bill said 'no way' to putting more cash into the franchise. I'm not sure of all the reasons why he said no, but by this time both the Sorianos and Daley had become targets of the local papers, who were quite aware of how badly things were going both on the field and behind the scenes on the inside. In fact, the *Seattle Times* had run a column titled something like 'Go Home, Mr. Daley,' by sportswriter Hy Zimmerman. So, Daley stayed with his money in Cleveland. He knew his baseball numbers, and they weren't adding up in Seattle." Daley's health may have also been an issue, as he died a short time later in 1971, reportedly after a long illness.

"It appeared by this time that we would be lucky to hit seven hundred thousand in attendance. We had projected one million. And for a cash-poor team with big loans and big park maintenance problems, no TV revenue, a mediocre radio contract, only a small percentage of concession revenue, and a sorry team with some shaky leadership in key positions, missing three hundred thousand paying fans was more than a problem. It was impending disaster."

Most don't remember that Seattle didn't rank last in the league in attendance, or even second to last. In fact, there were four teams in the MLB with worse attendance in 1969. The Pilots actually outdrew the Chicago White Sox, the Cleveland Indians, the Philadelphia Phillies, and the San Diego Padres. But they didn't have any of the other revenue advantages the established teams in the league had, such as higher concession revenue and much higher TV and radio revenue, and lower maintenance costs. For Seattle, hitting their attendance mark was far more critical. It didn't happen.

Bob continued, "Meanwhile, just to keep things interesting, a married player-personnel employee, another of the early administrative hires, got in a car wreck using a company car. He was rumored to be going out with one of the secretaries. Slightly hurt and obviously embarrassed, he wasn't coming in to work. Dewey got suspicious when he didn't show up for work for a couple of days, but I don't think any disciplinary action ever occurred at the time, but it was another key administrator on shaky ground."

Jim conceded that "we had a few guys on the juice." There's no confirmation that was the case in this embarrassing incident, but the optics weren't good. And everyone knew "Dewey was really down on people who couldn't handle their alcohol," Jim continued. "I think I used to get invited to staff events and parties just because I didn't drink and could be the designated driver for whomever might need it the most . . . those affairs always ended up with a number of people having way too much to drink."

Except for this incident, the player-personnel administrator was reportedly a capable guy. But it was clear he occasionally lacked focus.

Some of these goings-on might help explain why Dick Bates, the young pitcher who was Lou Piniella's spring training roommate and who had "the best spring training I ever had," and made the opening day team, was sent down after pitching only 1 2/3 innings. The twenty-two-year-old got hit around a bit in his only appearance but struck out three guys, then was simply informed he was being sent down to AAA Vancouver [British Columbia] . . . and was never heard from in Seattle again. Or maybe it's better put to say that the Pilots never talked to him again. His career minor league numbers included a 3.60 earned run average in 946 innings, with a 1.30 career WHIP ratio (walks plus hits to innings pitched), while giving up only 883 hits in those 946 innings, a very good ratio.

Bates, who, ironically, was originally signed in 1964 by Kansas City, where his spring training roommate, Piniella, ended up, did stay with Milwaukee in 1970, mostly in AA ball, where he posted a strong 3.87 earned run average with an excellent 1.22 WHIP at the age of twenty-four. That was his last year in the game. In today's much more scientifically impacted and analytics-oriented game, it's commonly known that twenty-six to thirty-two are typically the prime years for a player, when youth, athleticism, and maturity all come together for the majority of players.

Tom Kelly was another of the Pilots farmhands floating around the system. Plucked out of high school by Seattle in the June 1968 draft as an eighth-round pick, he never made much of a dent as a player. He didn't get an extended shot in the major leagues despite an impressive career batting average of .271 with a .405 career on-base percentage over thirteen minor league years. Kittilsby, who enrolled Kelly at Mesa Community College to keep him from getting drafted and also cosigned the contract for Kelly's first car, said, "I never envisioned Kelly would later win two World Series titles as a manager for the Minnesota Twins."

Bob Lemon, now a Hall of Fame pitcher, was manager of the AAA team in Vancouver, which had a number of Pilots minor leaguers. He was one of those who often had a little too much to drink, for which he was once admonished by former GM Edo Vanni, although Bob was not a witness to any of that.[3]

"I was asked to go pick up Bob Lemon in Vancouver and bring him back to Seattle for a meeting. I had never met him before, if my memory serves. On the way from Vancouver to Seattle in the car, Lemon was good-naturedly giving my wife a bad time for reading in the stands during the Vancouver baseball game," recalled Schoenbachler. There were only small crowds averaging 850 fans per game up there that year.

"Our seats were placed on the first base line, just a few rows up from the field, and the Vancouver dugout was along the third base line, so Bob Lemon could see us quite clearly and noticed she was reading and not paying any attention to the game at all. Lemon was probably a little agitated about it. He told my wife she was too used to major league crowds where that kind of stuff wouldn't be noticed."

As it turns out, Kittilsby, already burdened with growing responsibilities on the team, instinctively began to gather more knowledge about minor league players elsewhere in the Seattle system. "I even kept my eye out for what my first mentor, Lew Matlin, jokingly called players with consistently bad attitudes as in, 'he's a red-ass, hard-noser perpetualous.'" Matlin had come to Seattle from the AAA Vancouver Mounties, where he had been general manager.

This growing interest in the players would set up a later date with destiny for Kittilsby in Arizona. He was first the instructional league coordinator after the 1968 AAA Seattle Angels transition season. Later, he was assigned to Arizona to coordinate spring training for what was then the Seattle Pilots, in February and March, before they abruptly became the Brewers in extended spring training in April 1970.

But before taking on the 1970 spring training duties, Kittilsby became involved in drafting players for Seattle in the June 1969 amateur high school and college player draft. "I didn't participate in determining who to draft, but the guys in scouting were so microphone shy and speaking-in-public shy that they asked me to make the announcements about who we drafted.

"Just to stay consistent with how the rest of the year was going, which was basically terrible, the Pilots drafted a pitcher named Pat Osborn. He had already been drafted a couple of times by other teams in previous years and didn't sign because he either wanted to stay in school and develop more, or he didn't want to sign because the bonus wasn't large enough, or both.

"Why we decided to pick a guy who already had given some indication that he wouldn't sign for a low bonus number, which is all the cash-poor Pilots had to offer, is beyond me. Sure enough, he didn't sign, so Seattle completely wasted an overall eleventh pick in the entire draft. But the good news is we had another pick at number twenty-one and signed Gorman Thomas, who ended up being a pretty good power hitter. The bad news is, he was a great power hitter for Milwaukee, not for the Pilots."

Jim remembers, "Despite missing on our first pick, my most memorable moment at that draft was not our first picks. It was the moment in the draft when one of the teams, I think it was San Francisco, announced 'The San Francisco Giants are selecting player X in the twelfth round of the Major League Baseball amateur draft.' From the back of the room came this response, 'That's too bad, Jack, because he died in an automobile accident two weeks ago. And he was a switch hitter, too.'

It was a surreal moment, but it brought the house down. Just like the season was going for us, it was very dark humor in the midst of a disaster."

Bob added, "By August, the Sorianos were running scared. Nothing seemed to be going right. At the same time, everyone had come to the conclusion that Marvin Milkes, the GM, was a screwed-up idiot, and no one would go near him, including me. Milkes became more and more unglued as time progressed, so I just dealt directly with the Sorianos. Dewey Soriano would at least listen, but frankly, although he knew the numbers, he was the public face and instinctive marketer at the top of the franchise. As a natural marketing guy, he preferred keeping things comfortably in the dark about how bad things were and was always positive in public. His brother Max had also had a bad break just a year earlier with an employee embezzlement problem at his bank, so I suspect more bad news about financial numbers with his baseball team wasn't something he wanted to dwell on."

"I'd say that bank issue ended up giving me my most unusual 'extra' responsibility," Kittilsby noted. "Max planted me on the bank board of directors and asked me to keep him informed of anything that might be coming up there."

A bit later in the season, as things looked worse, the Sorianos moved Bob Schoenbachler and his two secretary-assistants to a private trailer. Bob said, "I think they didn't want anybody looking over my shoulder at the numbers. Max Soriano would always come to see me and talk about numbers and reports. Even though everyone could feel that we were in trouble, I was the only one that really knew our exact position because I was seeing the numbers every day. I only dealt with the Sorianos, though, although believe me, I was constantly asked by nearly everyone, 'What's going on?'

"We got a brief reprieve from bad attendance early in August with the 'bat day,' giving away free bats to fans. The stands were unexpectedly jam-packed, and that was a surprise because it was also Seafair weekend, when the hydroplane races on nearby Lake Washington took place. At that time Seafair was probably *the* biggest annual attraction in the entire region. We thought that would draw people away from the game, especially on a nice day, and the exact opposite happened. It was our biggest crowd of the season.

"Of course, that means we were also unprepared, and what should have been a great day turned out to hurt our public image even further. We had only ordered enough bats for a crowd half the size, anticipating Seafair would draw large numbers of our fans to that event. As a result, lots of people who thought they were getting a bat didn't get one."

Jim Kittilsby relates about the same bat day game: "By that time, I was also responsible for ordering a lot of the special promotional materials, including in this case, the bats. Our promotions purchaser had been fired. Unfortunately, looking at previous attendance and the fact we had a major event as a competitor that day, I just made a call that turned out to be incorrect . . . by a big amount."

In a volunteer role that day as disappointed batless fans left the stadium, Bob was on the receiving end of trying to make things work out.

Explained Bob, "In a state of panic over fans being disappointed, we somehow foolishly decided it would be a good idea to stand near exits and make sure no one left the stadium with more than one bat, even though we advertised a bat for every fan. Our thinking, if you can call it that, was that we would ask for the extra bat(s) a family might be carrying and then give those bats to a family leaving the stadium who had no bat. If we couldn't give them a repatriated bat, we'd give them a business card with instructions to contact us later for a bat.

"Near the gates, several of us posted ourselves. We soon spotted a young teenager with three or four bats. Being dutiful, I approached him and asked for the bats back, except for one. He responded by saying, 'These belong to my brothers.' Looking around and not seeing anything that appeared to be his family, I replied, 'Well, then, where are they.' He said, 'They're already outside.' I asked him to go get them. Within a couple of minutes he returned with three younger teenagers, all African American. The original teen was white. Obviously not believing him, I responded, 'You've got to be kidding me.' He responded with a sad face, 'I can't help it if my mom married a black man.' At which point we returned the bats to the boys. Embarrassed as hell, I spent the next several minutes hiding in the Pilot offices so I didn't have to question people anymore as they left the stadium with multiple bats."

Kittilsby, too, improvised a solution: "As it became obvious that we didn't have anywhere near enough bats, I ran in to the office and handwrote many short notes, signed by me personally, that said something like, 'This person is entitled to one bat from the Seattle Pilots bat day event' and signed my name. I ran out to the exit gate and handed out the hurriedly made notes as disgruntled fans were leaving without bats. Really embarrassing. And, of course, we relived the embarrassment all season long as one by one those folks came back over time and asked for their bat. We had to order a lot more bats. It was a promotion gone bad."

In spite of the foiled attempts to make things right, both men recall feeling curiously on a temporary high. "We thought this attendance number might signal the start of a run of good attendance with the good weather, which could save the franchise. We thought it might buy us some needed time. That idea lasted only a couple of days, as attendance dropped back below projections almost immediately, and gloom settled in once again," Schoenbachler said.

Said Kittilsby: "We kept trying other, smaller promotions, like handing out player photos, trinkets, even pantyhose on

'Ladies Nites.' All hands were on deck for all of those promotions, with me, Bob, and other front-office personnel manning the gates."

Nothing seemed to click, though.

"I don't think GM Marvin Milkes was too impressed with our promotional efforts. As a do-everything GM in those days, he had often been involved at the minor league level in helping develop promotions himself. He would pull me aside, with maybe one or two others, and regale us with stories of his promotional genius. One of his stories was that he was able to sell an outfield billboard fence space to a mortuary, and helped them decide on the wording, which he said was 'You call, we haul, that's all.' Those of us who heard him tell that story more than once were pretty skeptical, especially because he always laughed at the end of the story.

"Another of Milkes's favorite stories about his ability to sell outfield billboard space was that he sold a billboard ad to an optometrist. He convinced the optometrist to place an eye chart with the big E at the top and smaller lines of letters as you read lower on the chart, and at about line three or four he intentionally had the painters start making the lines of little letters blurry. He was sure people in the stands would think their own eyes were going bad and go into the optometrist who was advertising on the sign. We were skeptical about that, too, but it was a lot more plausible than 'You call, we haul, that's all.'

"Little did we know that our bat day, which turned out to be iffy in itself, was just a sign of more chaos to come. Inevitably, we knew the end was near as promotion after promotion pretty much fizzled, but we didn't know exactly how or when the end would come."

11

Searching for Home Plate

By late August, speculation was rampant about whether the Pilots would survive in Seattle. Attendance, the key source of income for sustainability, was obviously much lower than anticipated, and the danger signals were loud and clear. The papers were on it; the radio voices were on it; the TV newscasters were on it.

Potential local buyers were popping up with some regularity, but most had the same problems as the Sorianos: they couldn't carry the huge loan balances, as they, too, were undercapitalized.

Meanwhile, the deep-pocketed co-owner from Cleveland had opted out of any further investment. The team still had less-than-needed radio revenue, no TV profit-sharing revenue, only 20 percent of concession revenue, and a stadium that was falling apart . . . on which they had to pay rent to the City of Seattle. Bank of California was not in a cooperating mood, either, sitting on an outstanding $4 million loan. They expected to be paid off as a part of any change in ownership.

One by one, local options were eliminated as the league reviewed proposals. One included the idea of a nonprofit team, but the other MLB team owners rejected that by one vote as the majority thought it might devalue their own teams. Other options included lovers of baseball, as the Sorianos were, but local proposals, one by one, fell short.

"Regretfully, I couldn't help the guy who first hired me in baseball, Edo Vanni," Bob recalls. "Edo kept asking me for financials on the Pilots as they continued to struggle; I think he was trying to put something together to buy the team. I told him he'd have to go to Dewey himself to get those. Edo said he couldn't do that, having already been demoted by Dewey, so I went to Dewey myself and asked if I could give Edo the financials. Dewey blew up and gave me a firm no, then later let Edo go in the end, probably one of our more positive administrators and baseball guys. I felt badly about that.

"Another local option was a local guy, Fred Danz, who seemed a little slick around the edges. Whenever he came around to discuss the team, he gave us all tickets to the theaters he owned, sort of acting like he was throwing money around like a big shot. Turns out when some of us used the tickets, there was a 'service charge' on them that he forgot to mention. Danz wanted to appear as if he had deep pockets, but with a little sniffing it was clear his 'deep pockets' weren't nearly deep enough to purchase the team. His 'free' tickets that weren't really free were a clue." Danz offered up a deal in November 1969, and his application was approved by the American League, but when it came time to put the money on the table, Danz either didn't have it or just decided not to do it. By December, that option was gone.

By late fall and heading into the dark of winter, it was becoming rather obvious that an owner outside of Seattle might be a distinct possibility, as local options looked shaky.

And with Seattle attendance below seven hundred thousand for the season, not a lot of locals were scrambling to invest.

One of the early outside options came from Dallas, Texas, but that option, too, quickly came and went. It's been suggested that the Houston offer "went" because MLB already had an option waiting in the wings, perhaps already tipped off to the precarious nature of the Seattle franchise.

The city of Milwaukee, which had lost their Braves to Atlanta after the 1965 season, kept popping up, along with the name of a car salesman, Bud Selig. In fact, he'd advanced far beyond being a car salesman . . . he owned a Milwaukee Ford dealership. His involvement looked increasingly like the real thing.

It's been reported that during the last few broadcast games of the Pilots, the announcers were asked to mention Milwaukee as a likely landing spot for the team, and to mention Seattle as little as possible.

Marketing maven Bill Sears came up with another branding tag behind the scenes, this time beginning to call the Seattle team late in the season the "Brewlots," a combination of the Brewers and the Pilots. Sears obviously kept his eyes and ears open.

Bob Schoenbachler also recalls telling his wife, "There's a chance the ball club could be sold and go elsewhere; and if I'm asked to go, I think we should go."

Jim recalls, "Marvin Milkes was pretty sure things were going downhill fast, too. He was always a basket case, but now he seemed even more paranoid. I remember he sidled over to me once and said, 'We probably aren't going to renew the contracts of the scouting and farm directors, so I don't want you eating with them. Eat at a different table.' Like I said, he worried about *everything*. And that meant two more administrators were going down at some point soon.

"In addition to worrying about everything, Marvin seemed not to trust anyone he hadn't hired himself, and that included everyone from the two guys he told me to not get too much more 'buddy-buddy' with because we weren't going to renew their contracts all the way to our two radio announcers. Milkes didn't think they were up to par, either. One announcer was hired by the Sorianos, and the other came from Cleveland on a recommendation from ownership partner Bill Daley. Milkes derisively called them the Bobbsey Twins after a popular children's book in his day about two sets of child twins. As for letting the two player-personnel guys go, I don't know if it was totally Milkes's call, as one of them was involved in the car crash with the secretary and the rumored drinking, and that stuff didn't sit well with Dewey Soriano."

In the end, after much legal maneuvering by Seattle to keep the team, and by Milwaukee to get the team, and by the American League to get something decided and done, a Milwaukee lawyer proposed the idea to Bud Selig and to the Sorianos of a bankruptcy. Teams of bankruptcy lawyers were brought into the fray.

Certified Bob, as the comptroller, was asked to testify before the bankruptcy court. "The hearings were difficult and a bit confusing, as Seattle was obviously not yet a well-established franchise. We first had to prove that the Pilots were, in fact, bankrupt and unable to carry on. Then, we had to make the case that the only viable offer to purchase the club was the Selig offer of $10.8 million. Both anticipated operating costs and franchise value were major issues.

"Our 'future revenue' was almost nonexistent, as we had an even lower radio contract offer for the new year and no TV contract, season ticket sales and advertising revenue amounted to almost nothing, and we were not scheduled to receive any revenue from the MLB Central Fund for another two years. And we still had huge maintenance problems with Sicks Stadium with no cash flow to address them.

"All of our ownership contracts with players we drafted from other teams were purchased at pretty much the same amount, the $175,000 we paid for purchasing each. That was all quite different than nearly every other major league team."

Bob remembers, "As player contracts for Pilot ownership were signed, the contracts were placed on the books at their ownership purchase price. I also testified that the player's annual playing contracts, separate from the ownership purchase price, were for their salaries, which was a business expense, not an asset. I submitted a recap of the one hundred forty-nine players the Pilots owned and the value of their ownership contracts at the time of the court case. Their ownership value, in our case almost always $175,000 per player plus anyone we signed on our own separate from the draft, we had planned to depreciate over five years."

Bob also showed 1969 operating costs, which were over $3.7 million, and submitted projections for the 1970 season showing that "there was not enough money to cover upcoming operating costs unless additional cash was injected into the company. We couldn't project that much revenue."

Throughout the proceedings, others also made the case that the money to continue running the Pilots just wasn't there, and wasn't likely to be there in any scenario, even "best-case." On top of that, Bank of California had called the $4 million loan, and there was no local buyer willing to step up with that over their heads.

Behind the scenes, at the time only rumored to be at the October World Series, the Sorianos, Bill Daley, and Bud Selig are said to have reached an understanding on a sale price, enough to cover the debt and then some. It is unlikely Selig would have done so without the knowledge of Major League Baseball. His earlier efforts to save the Milwaukee Braves and later to buy the Chicago White Sox as a replacement probably worked in his favor, as he had already gone through a vetting process and developed several inside relationships.

In an interview years later with Mike Fuller of SeattlePilots.com, who in 1994 held a series of remarkable interviews with the various inside parties involved, Dewey Soriano confirmed the World Series meetings and outlined what actually happened with those October negotiations:

"We had been negotiating with Milwaukee in the latter part of the 1969 season, because we knew that the ball club had to be moved in order to pay the debts of the club.

"We entered into a gentlemen's agreement at the World Series in late October of '69. The Mets were playing the Baltimore Orioles there at the Baltimore park. At the second game of the series, we concluded a deal with Bud Selig and Mr. [Edmund] Fitzgerald, who was the senior man there at the negotiations. We had made this gentlemen's agreement for the acquisition by Milwaukee—if the American League would allow the transfer of the team, which was absolutely essential.

"We had gone to Mr. Cronin and told him of this, and he said, 'Well, we have to set up a special meeting,' which they did in Chicago. The American League owners met in Chicago with the Milwaukee contingent not present. They set up a committee to investigate the situation in Seattle and report back to the league just as soon as possible. Because this was October and they wanted to be able to finalize something as soon as they could. The committee, I believe, was made up of four different owners.

"The committee came back three weeks to a month later—in the middle of November—and said that 'by all means, the present owners of the Pilots should try to obtain ownership in Seattle for the club. That the club could not and should not be transferred.' They wanted Seattle to get a fair deal, that every effort should be made to keep the club in Seattle. That was a strong effort by the American League. They said flatly, 'No, you can't move that club. Seattle has not had a fair chance, and we're not in the business of putting a franchise in a city and then after one year, transferring it out.' They were adamant about it, even though we had discussed some of the shortfalls of the stadium and so forth."[1]

Meanwhile, speculation continued to run rampant, both on a national level and in Seattle, where General Manager Marvin Milkes was still saying publicly that the team would be in Seattle in 1970. As late as March 8, 1970, the *New York Times* reported on the issue, including this:

> The American League may yet move its Seattle franchise to Milwaukee in time for the 1970 baseball season, just one month away, despite a decision three weeks ago to keep the Pilots in Seattle partly subsidized by the other 11 teams. A meeting of the league's owners in Tampa on Tuesday will settle the issue one way or another.
>
> Discussion about moving the Pilots has been going on since last October, when Bill Daley, the principal owner, made tentative agreement to sell the club to a Milwaukee group. Subsequently, a Dallas group including Lamar Hunt made a strong bid, while Seattle and State of Washington officials threatened an antitrust suit and Congressional action if the team were not kept in Seattle.
>
> Reluctant to face such a suit, and public criticism for abandoning a new city after only one year of operation, the other club owners tried to find a purchaser for the club in Seattle. Two such attempts fell through, and on Feb.

10 and 11, in Chicago, it was decided to let Daley's group continue to operate the club in Seattle with $650,000 to be contributed by the other 11 teams in the league to meet current expenses.

Now, however, some of those who accepted this plan are having second thoughts. As more specific arithmetic is done about the probable losses in Seattle this year, and with no clear prospect of success in the future, there is a growing feeling against throwing "good money after bad."[2]

Essentially, the American League came to the same conclusion as Bill Daley had when he refused to invest more money to save the Pilots. Putting more money into the Pilots didn't seem like a viable option or a smart investment. It turns out that Daley was more right than wrong, despite being vilified in the Seattle press.

It would take awhile, and some maneuvering through court, to have the bankruptcy deal come to fruition. On at least one occasion, the Sorianos, through their lead bankruptcy lawyer, Wally Aiken, called the judge and greased the wheels a bit, as it were. As Bob, who was in the room for one call, remembers, "The message was 'we are going to present such-and-such, and for this to work, you'll need to rule this, this, and this.' Whether this was simply to just keep the judge informed, or to urge the judge to make a certain decision, or indications of an insider deal on which there was common agreement, is anyone's guess."

At the bankruptcy hearing, General Manager Milkes testified there was not enough money to pay the coaches, players, and office staff. He told the court that if he was more than ten days late in paying the players, "the players will all become free agents and leave Seattle without a team for the 1970 season." The urgency to make a decision was increasing.

The Pilots ended the year over $8 million in debt. Any cash flow had disappeared in the futile attempt to save a franchise that from the start would be doomed should anything go wrong. Obviously, several "anythings" contributed to the final outcome.

Federal Bankruptcy Referee Sidney Volinn declared the Pilots bankrupt.

Volinn, too, was interviewed by Mike Fuller in 1994.

> Fuller: "Did it make any difference that William Daley had the financial means to put in more money or that the American League had pledged $650,000 to keep the team going in Seattle after they rejected Eddie Carlson's nonprofit proposal?"
>
> Volinn: "I just felt that, to put it crudely, 'a bird in the hand is worth two in the bush.' There was $10 million there. It was going to pay everybody and that's all we knew. We also knew that there were possibilities that somebody else could take care of these debts, but they were only possibilities, and the possibility of bailing out the Pilots had been discussed for months.

"The financial problems of the Pilots by the time we had this hearing were well known and had been well known by people on the inside for a long, long time. The Sorianos themselves had been desperately exploring for a long, long time, getting the funds to keep themselves together.

"I still remember Max Soriano—his appearance, he was so troubled. His brother, Dewey, at least on the outside was a more pragmatic-looking individual. You could see in Mr. Soriano's posture and his appearance as this thing developed over the weeks, he really was under an enormous stress and very troubled. It was not a good time for the Soriano brothers. It was a very bad time. The public pressures were tremendous, their responsibilities were great and they were aware of it and they just couldn't raise the money. They were trying desperately.

"There I was sitting there, evaluating, and I just felt for the people directly involved and, indeed, in the long-range public interest, the best thing to do was to take the offer. There it was. There was nothing else that came anywhere near it. There was no prospect of anything else anywhere near it. What was there was chaos."[3]

On this point, as many others have attested, there was common agreement.

About the only one associated with the Seattle team destined to come out on top in this deal was Jim Bouton, whose book, *Ball Four*, was a huge seller. "Well, Bouton and the grounds-crew guy who got all of Milkes's new shirts," Bob laughed. "I guess they both made out OK."

Earlier, Major League Baseball sent in their own selected administrators to help facilitate a smooth transition and protect their asset during the last few months of the Pilots and before the opening of the new season in 1970. Most Pilots staff were let go in late 1969 or early 1970 or were finding other options as grim reality became unavoidable.

Finally, with the handwriting on the wall but the bankruptcy proceedings not yet finalized, Dewey Soriano met with all the staff that remained. "We aren't going to make it. And I'm sorry to say we don't have money to pay you. You can leave if you want to, that's certainly understandable. Or, if you prefer, you can stay here and work with us as we close down, but it will have to be without pay."

Edo Vanni was in the room, one of those being let go. Having already sensed what was up, and perhaps not too happy with how he had been treated both in the hiring of Marvin

Milkes and in his quest for more financial information about the team, Edo had come prepared with a rubber laughing toy in his pocket. As Dewey turned and walked out the door and others started to leave, Edo stuck his hand in his pocket and turned on the laughing machine.

True to his wife's description, even in the end Edo appeared to be seeking a fight in an empty room.

At the same time, Edo knew his team and supported his team members. Those still in the vicinity broke out laughing, and the dour mood was lifted. Most of those still remaining had pretty much seen what was coming, and decided to see it out to the end, without pay.

After being left adrift by the Pilots, Edo Vanni retired from baseball, although for years after he carried the title of "Dean of Seattle baseball." He was known for his sharp memory of details stretching over thirty-five years of high school, college, and minor league baseball. He played, he managed, and he was part of administration, so his stories were varied, legion, and funny. He met players on the way up and met many of them on the way back down. But his last memory of his Pilots experience was this, recalled in an interview with Larry Stone of the *Seattle Times* in 2005: "When major-league baseball finally came here in 1969, Vanni served in the front office of the short-lived Seattle Pilots, all one year of it—'the biggest farce I ever saw,' Vanni said."[4]

"In the very end, I was about the only staff left in Seattle," Bob recalls, "and Jim was about the only staff person left in Arizona. I was receiving all the bankruptcy court paperwork in Seattle and providing documents to the court, while Jim was in Arizona receiving instructions on what to do next, often from the same bankruptcy court."

On March 31, 1970, just days before the start of the new season, the Seattle team that had been training in Arizona for Seattle Pilot season number two was declared bankrupt and awarded to Milwaukee and Bud Selig. Selig had reached a deal with the Sorianos to buy the team for $10.8 million. The news hit the papers the next day. Like it had when it traded soon-to-be Rookie of the Year Lou Piniella to the competing Kansas City expansion team a year to the day earlier, Seattle was to suffer another April Fools' joke, to the city's detriment and embarrassment.

Thousands of printed 1970 Seattle Pilots schedules and the 1970 press book were headed toward the trash bin or were sent to Milwaukee to be used by the new Brewers, since they couldn't get new ones printed in time for opening day. Today the few remaining are treasured by collectors of Pilots memorabilia.

Bud Selig had made a perfect pitch, and Seattle had struck out.

The investors in the club, including the Sorianos and Bill Daley, got their investment back from the bankruptcy sale, and bills and loans were paid for other services already rendered, but there was little left. Especially for the headaches and heartaches endured, no one took a lot of money to the bank on the Seattle end of the deal.

The last pitch by an actual Seattle Pilot was thrown on October 2, 1969. Attendance was 5,473. Young rookie Miguel Fuentes, called up at season's end after a strong minor league campaign, with high hopes and expectations for his future in Seattle, threw the last pitch of the last game for the Pilots. As fortune would have it, it was his last pitch, as well.

During the off-season, Miguel Fuentes was murdered in a bar fight at the age of twenty-three. The last Seattle Pilot to grace the mound.

12

April Fools' Déjà Vu: New Town, New Team, New Problems

Jim Kittilsby, working in Arizona as the assistant to general manager Marvin Milkes, and now the executive secretary of scouting, was also the coordinator of Seattle's 1970 spring training. The Seattle Pilots' equipment trucks, in Arizona since February, were packed up from spring training at the end of March and driven north to Provo, Utah. Parked, the trucks' drivers awaited instructions to go either northwest to Seattle, or northeast to Milwaukee. On April 1, April Fools' Day, learning of the March 31 decision, they were instructed to head northeast to Milwaukee.

It was not Kittilsby who gave the drivers their instructions, though. No one on Seattle's management team thought to call him after the court decision. He learned of the decision from the radio. "At that point, I was down in Arizona by myself with remaining players not assigned to any team," Kittilsby said. "My secretary had already been let go. I was sitting in the office from about six a.m. until late in the evening frantically working on player releases, and no one called me. Finally, I heard on the radio sports news that Seattle had been declared bankrupt and sold to Milwaukee."

There is more irony in the transition to Milwaukee than most realize. In the entire history of baseball, only one other team lasted just one year in a city. Curiously, that team was the 1901 Milwaukee Brewers, who in 1902, though not prompted by bankruptcy, became the St. Louis Browns. Today they are the Baltimore Orioles.[1]

In 1969, the Seattle Pilots ended the year over $8 million in debt. "Fifty years later, I don't recall the debt number exactly; it could have been much more," Bob noted.

The Sorianos were financially saved by the Brewers deal, but they and the city of Seattle were devastated by the failure. Seattle had been one of the best minor league cities in baseball for over seventy years, dating as far back as the late 1800s. From the 1950s through the late 1960s, Seattle was at or near the top of minor league attendance for fifteen straight seasons. Now, they were left with no team at all, a fate unimaginable just twelve months earlier.

Major league baseball, as well as a long history of minor league baseball, was done in Seattle after one fateful year. It was a victim of hurried decision-making prompted by the Kansas City team moving to Oakland, and Major League Baseball's need for a balanced schedule, among a host of other things. A team in Seattle far earlier than anyone was prepared for was also a team leaving far earlier than anyone could have imagined.

Just as MLB's decision to jump-start the Seattle Pilots created an entirely unanticipated and disastrous set of problems that brought down the franchise, the move to Milwaukee had the potential to do the same.

With Milwaukee learning it had landed the team just days before the season began, the team had no proper uniforms, only a vague idea of which players were going where in the system, no ongoing ticket sales, little staffing, and no built-in transition teams to coordinate between the outgoing Pilots and the incoming Brewers.

Jim Kittilsby, the soft-spoken, broadly experienced, and widely trusted administrator, had been asked to handle things in Arizona at the 1970 spring training site. He had already administered the Pilots' fall instructional league after the minor league seasons had ended for Seattle. In the late spring of 1970, the few still working for the team, including Bob Schoenbachler, were still in Seattle, mostly spending time in a courtroom.

"I was alone doing everything by hand down there, including paying about a hundred and fifty players by handwritten checks and making three copies of each of the checks to send to Seattle, Milwaukee, and the bankruptcy court," Kittilsby said. "I had to do this every week. On top of that, I was told to change banks at least three times by the bankruptcy referee, and so I had to get blank checks from the new bank each time, counter checks that had no addresses on them, so I had to handwrite the address on every single check, too."

Kittilsby was now also the one doing the releasing of Pilots players not being added to the Milwaukee organization. He was getting conflicting information (and at various times too much or not enough information) from the Pilots, and from Major League Baseball. In addition to oversight provided by the bankruptcy court, MLB had assigned some Yankees administrators to work the transition to protect its investment. Another layer of "oversight and instruction" was added once Milwaukee was confirmed as the new owner.

"The first thing I did was fill out the AAA-, AA-, and A-level rosters with players Milwaukee wanted to keep. Then, as is common, those not yet assigned were asked to work out in an extended spring training. It was disappointing for all those remaining, but also their last hope, so many stayed, disappointed and increasingly disgruntled.

"The extended spring training took us through opening day of 1970, now in Milwaukee. I took a plane to Milwaukee for opening day, met my new secretary for the first time, stayed for the game and did some start-up organizational work for a day or two, then hopped back on a plane for Arizona.

"Upon my return, it was clear to every remaining player that they weren't going to be in the Milwaukee organization. It was my job, though, to make that formal, and inform them.

"The mass release of so many players to this day is the biggest single-day release of players in modern baseball history," Jim recalls. "That's not something to brag about, but it's a fact. Thirty-six players were given their disposition notice at the same time.

"Back then, normally players were released little by little as spring training progressed and daily meetings held to give a thumbs-up or thumbs-down on players. Typically, if someone spoke up on behalf of a player, he was saved for another day. But if the next day he went 0–4 with an error, or something like that, and his name came up the next day and nobody came to his rescue, he was gone. So, day by day, this had been happening throughout the spring.

"But we had come to the end of spring training, all of our players we wanted to keep had been assigned, and there was nowhere to put the remaining thirty-six. This was especially true because Seattle no longer had any minor league teams, and the Milwaukee minor league system was still being worked out. I had to call the National Association of Professional Baseball Leagues, basically the headquarters for minor league baseball administration, and announce they were all being released that day. I remember the response on the other end of the line: 'Geez, Jim, this is an all-time record. Never in the history of the minor leagues have this many players ever been released on the same day by the same team.' Baseball keeps records of everything; their 'who did this the most, who did that the most' stuff is almost like a Ripley's Believe It or Not! thing. But I'm hoping my name is nowhere to be found on that one.

"The hotel bus driver was instructed to ensure every player had all their stuff as they boarded the team bus from the hotel to the minor league stadium in Tempe. I didn't want them to go back to their living quarters, some in a hotel, others in an Arizona State University rented dorm, and mess up the place in their anger. They were given their release and enough airfare to get them from Tempe to the airport nearest their hometown, and taken directly to the airport.

"When they got off the plane, they were totally on their own. Most of those players entered spring training with the expectation of being somewhere in Seattle's minor league system, and now they were entirely out of baseball. Seattle didn't have a team, and therefore had no minor league system."

Fortunately, Kittilsby had developed a relationship with most of the players throughout the spring. In fact, among his several nicknames was "The Man of La Mancha" because the dorm in which he had housed many of them on the Arizona State University campus was called La Mancha.

"To make matters more confusing," Jim continued, "right in the middle of preparing for the disposition process, I was contacted by a Milwaukee attorney. He told me to 'quit disposing of our assets,' meaning the players I was letting go from the Seattle organization. But Seattle had nowhere to assign them, Milwaukee hadn't assigned them to a minor league team, they were no longer on a valid contract, and they had to get home. Bud Selig finally called and said to release the players."

In addition to Seattle Pilots instructions, MLB instructions, bankruptcy court instructions, and Milwaukee instructions, local Arizona attorneys also started getting in on the act to tell Jim what to do.

"There was a local Arizona developer who had a development deal with the Sorianos for commercial and residential development around the Arizona complex, and had already sunk costs into the development. Milwaukee wasn't going to accept that deal as part of the bankruptcy proceeding, and the developer, E. B. Smith, was rightfully concerned that they wouldn't be getting their money back if the Pilots went under.

"Smith was trying to get his hands on the gate receipts for spring training games. Earlier, he had the gates locked on a day we had a game scheduled, but we got the locks off and played the game. In any event, Smith appeared to have pull with the local sheriff, as he tried to have me arrested in Tempe for 'misappropriation of funds.'"

Jim had been taking directions from the bankruptcy court in Seattle, the court apparently aware that others might be trying to get their hands on whatever assets were still liquid. The bankruptcy court instructions included having Jim change the banks holding the funds he was using in Tempe to run the Arizona operation.

Jim found himself confronted upon arriving to work on "getaway day," the day all the players were leaving. He was unable to get in to continue the already difficult and tense process of wrapping things up, and literally closing things down, just as he had in Tacoma years before. In Tempe at the complex, a sheriff's deputy was waiting with a warrant for his arrest.

"I didn't know what was going on, since no one had warned me. I just showed up to work, and they were ready to put me in handcuffs and take me to jail. I had to talk fast, as the players had to get to the airport and I also had a charter plane waiting to take me to Milwaukee.

"The Maricopa County Sheriff's officials were surprised to learn I was taking instruction from the bankruptcy court and under court orders. After some very awkward discussion, they let me go, and I don't think they were happy that they had not been fully informed by Smith.

"I was just as surprised it was E. B. Smith again, because I had both dinner and several lunches with him, and thought we were on good terms and that he understood that the issue had to go through bankruptcy court. We didn't talk again after that stunt. I was told he was crooked, but as far as I knew that was just rumor and speculation.

"Just like the start of the year for the Pilots, the end was the same . . . a fiasco."

As the Seattle Pilots faded into oblivion in the west, Jim had the same decision to make as the truck drivers with all the spring training equipment. Head west, or head east for Milwaukee?

Jim headed east.

He had already talked with his old alma mater, Pacific Lutheran University, about a multiposition role there, starting in the summer of 1970 "whenever he was ready to make the transition" according to his PLU contact. He agreed to stay with Milwaukee until July 1, taking them through the June draft of college and high school players.

His new title was executive secretary of scouting and assistant to the general manager, with a new team, the Milwaukee Brewers. He arrived in time to see the Pilots insignias being taken off the uniforms that had just arrived, see Milwaukee Brewers insignias sewn onto the old Seattle uniforms, and watch the old uniforms take their positions on a different field in a new city.

But this time, at least, he didn't have to model the uniform for publicity shots.

13

Things Warm Up in Milwaukee

Not quite twenty-three, Bob Schoenbachler was asked to stay on and be a part of the Milwaukee Brewers as their comptroller. He and the mercurial and widely disliked Seattle general manager Marvin Milkes, who had another year to go on his contract, were the first to hop on a plane and head for Milwaukee.

The Milwaukee team was to open the season on April 7, 1970, just days away. The team's equipment and uniforms were slowly being trucked from their temporary holding place in Utah, most all of it branded with the Seattle Pilots logo.

Curiously, Schoenbachler and Milkes were sent to different hotels in Milwaukee: Bob to the Schroeder, and Milkes to the Pfister. Two feet of snow was on the ground when their flight landed in Milwaukee.

Despite the heavy snowfall, Bud Selig greeted them at the airport to accompany them to their hotels.

"Bud Selig is a fantastic baseball guy," says Bob. "Tommy Ferguson told me he used to walk around as a kid with a transistor radio to his ear and do nothing but listen to baseball. He won more than a few friendly bets playing baseball trivia. Bud was like a walking, talking encyclopedia of baseball. He loved telling people that the last game Babe Ruth ever played was *not* with the Yankees, but with the National League Boston Braves, who later became the Milwaukee Braves."

Bob continued, "Selig also was on top of the financials, good with numbers. They didn't call him 'Budget Bud' for nothing. Unlike Dewey Soriano, Bud was quite good with numbers, wanted to know them, [was] aware of them always, and made budget-conscious decisions."

"I'm not sure Bud knew my nickname was Certified Bob back in Seattle, as that time had passed a bit. But I did know my stuff when testifying at bankruptcy court in Seattle. It might have given him some comfort to know that while I was young, I had that kind of a good, reliable reputation and got my figures right."

Selig was born in Milwaukee and grew up in a Jewish family. His father was an immigrant born in Romania who came to the United States when he was four. But Bud Selig's interest in baseball came from his mother at a very early age. She was an immigrant from Ukraine, and became a schoolteacher in the United States, with a college degree. She began taking Bud and his brother, Jerry, to minor league games as kids.

When the Boston Braves major league team moved to Milwaukee in 1953, Selig committed to them heart and soul as the Milwaukee Braves, so much so that as he grew older he used his increasing wealth from the automobile business to become, by 1963, the team's largest public stockholder. The Braves then left Milwaukee for Atlanta in 1966, an effort that Selig fought to prevent, and lost. Selig then sold his Braves stock and took on the task of bringing another major league team to Milwaukee.

In fact, the Seattle Pilots were not Selig's first target. He attempted to buy the Chicago White Sox and reached an agreement with them in early 1969, only to be rebuffed by the American League. Chicago was America's second largest city at the time, and the American League wanted to keep an American League team there.[1] But his previous part ownership of the Braves, and the process of negotiation and fact-finding and developing relationships with other owners in the attempt to purchase the White Sox, very likely greased the wheels on the Seattle deal. When it came time, Selig was able to make an inside pitch to the other owners, who by that time knew him well.

Bob, transitioning from Seattle, was unsure how long he would be with Milwaukee. "When we went to Milwaukee, a lot of it was on good faith. Several of us didn't have actual contracts; none of us had yet been given titles. We just went to work doing whatever had to be done, not knowing if we would have a permanent job after everything settled following the transition period."

By the end of the year, however, Bob was given the title of comptroller and assistant treasurer of the new Milwaukee Brewers by Selig. It was another move up in Bob's unusually rapid ascent in Major League Baseball.

Only a little over forty-eight months earlier, Schoenbachler had been working on his car in a local garage south of Seattle as a teenager, then attending business school. Having quit his first accounting job, and out of a combination of necessity and curiosity, at age nineteen he had applied for a vaguely worded job description as auditor for a baseball team, a job he'd just seen posted on a placement board at his community college. He had never played baseball or worked for a team or even seen a major league game. He hadn't even yet obtained an accounting degree. Yet here he was, four years later, comptroller and assistant treasurer with the new Milwaukee Brewers. As he readied for opening day 1970, he remembered that just a year earlier, he was readying for opening day with a different new major league team, the Seattle Pilots. By the end of 1971 he would be promoted to treasurer–assistant secretary for the Brewers, and by 1972 promoted again to secretary-treasurer. He would reach "grizzled veteran" status by the age of twenty-five.

Nonetheless, Schoenbachler and Kittilsby agreed that opening day in Milwaukee was almost as chaotic as opening day in Seattle had been, but without the Seattle disaster of seats still being under construction as fans arrived.

"I immediately started organizing things in the ticket office," Schoenbachler recalled. "There was a foot of snow on the ground, and it's the first week in April. My instructions were 'Stay here and clean up this mess.' People in Milwaukee were excited and rushing in to buy tickets. I had been rushed out from Seattle and had no winter clothes, so I was freezing my ass off.

"We had no farm teams for the first couple of weeks of the season; they were still being set up. We had no computers [it was 1970; desktops and laptops were years away], no office supplies, no adding machines. All the work was being done on paper worksheets.

"I even had to go to the store the day before opening day to get all kinds of supplies, including spreadsheets and accounting forms, plus we had to hire a secretary and a payroll person, set up a payroll system for staff and players, and find out with accuracy who our players were, and set up the formal roster. We were only eight days out from our first player payroll, and we didn't yet know for sure who our players were, who would be paying them, or how much we would be paying them. I don't know how the heck we did it, thinking back on it."

The night before Milwaukee's opening day had some eerie similarities to Seattle a year earlier, in that critical things were still being literally put together with no time to spare. In Seattle, the bleachers and scoreboards were being built through the night and into the morning of opening day. In Milwaukee a year later, seamstresses were hastily hired, and as game time approached, they were still removing Pilot patches and sewing new Milwaukee patches on the old Pilot uniforms. The Brewers took the field on opening day in obviously made-over Pilots uniforms. The son of one of the seamstresses remembers that his sandlot team took the field wearing the old Seattle Pilots patches, sewn on by team moms, quite a long fall from Major League Baseball in a single year.

Milwaukee made two quick hires that, unlike several of the early hires in Seattle, paid dividends. The first was a ticket manager from the White Sox who knew what he was doing, Dick Hackett. "It really helped take some of the immediate pressure off, having that organized," Schoenbachler said.

The second hire was Selig's own secretary, a move that unintentionally further cemented Schoenbachler's growing reputation with Bud Selig. The owner had asked Bob to do the interviewing for him and make a recommendation.

Schoenbachler, who was now called "Bobby" by Selig and hence by everyone else, hired one Lori Keck. She happened to have been revered Green Bay Packers' football coach Vince Lombardi's secretary before he died.

Selig was floored to learn that Keck had been with Vince Lombardi. His response: "You've *got* to be kidding me!" It turns out Lombardi was one of Selig's biggest sports heroes. Schoenbachler, of course, already knew this. He figured Bud would be impressed and pleased to have a secretary with such a great background serving a high-level public figure . . . a sports hero, no less.

"That really made me the fair-haired boy," Schoenbachler recalled. "Lori turned out to be a great secretary, and when Bud went on to become commissioner, Lori went with him to the commissioner's office. We needed someone to protect him, screen his calls and drop-in visitors, and she was great at it. Guys like Mitch Miller of 'follow the bouncing ball' orchestra fame used to come by and just stick their head in office doors, including mine, and talk. Lori got those things under better control, made things flow more smoothly, and made Bud a much better and more efficient administrator."

One way they all got through the chaos of opening in such a short time frame was that Selig "remained calm and steady, and left us alone to do our work."

The fact that Selig had been closely associated with the former Milwaukee Braves helped a lot. He was able to provide knowledgeable guidance without panic. That several of his new Brewers administrative team had gone through much the same thing in Seattle the year before gave them confidence they could get it done.

"It took only about three weeks for things to start settling in. Things had never settled in, in Seattle, there were just too many negatives from the start. After things calmed down in Milwaukee, some of the other owners and investors began to come around. It was obvious Bud had asked them to stay invisible until he thought a reasonable level of order was established.

"The first big investor I met was Oscar Mayer Jr.," Bob recalls. "I was walking down the hallway with Bud, he's walking down the hallway toward us. Bud stops to introduce me. To this day I can't remember a thing he said . . . and didn't remember then, either . . . because I couldn't get their advertising song out of my head as he was talking! 'I wish I was an Oscar Mayer wiener, that is what I really want to be. Because if I were an Oscar Mayer wiener, everyone would be in love with me.' I think I had a big grin on my face as he was talking.

"I also met owner Ed Fitzgerald early on. He was CEO of Cutler-Hammer. An iron-carrying ship named the *Edmund Fitzgerald* is the one that famously sank in Lake Superior about which a popular song was written, 'The Wreck of the *Edmund Fitzgerald*,' sung by Canadian Gordon Lightfoot." The ship was named after Mr. Fitzgerald's father, who was president and chairman of the board for Northwestern Mutual, which owned it."

Bob continued, "The story of the *Edmund Fitzgerald* is a fascinating one; I recently looked it up on the internet. Here's what it said." He had printed the story out:

> More than 15,000 people attended [the] *Edmund Fitzgerald*'s christening and launch ceremony on June 7, 1958. But the event was plagued by misfortunes: When Elizabeth Fitzgerald, wife of Edmund Fitzgerald, tried to christen the ship by smashing a champagne bottle over the bow, it took her three attempts to break it. A delay of 36 minutes followed while the shipyard crew struggled to release the keel blocks. Upon sideways launch, the ship created a large wave that 'doused' the spectators and then crashed into a pier before righting herself. One man watching the launching had a heart attack and later died.[2]

Bob continued, "In some ways that story reminds me of the entire Seattle Pilots experience. Like the *Edmund Fitzgerald*, we were star-crossed from the beginning. Nothing went right before the season even started, our team struggled to get everything right before the launch, nothing went right when the Pilots set sail during the season, nearly everyone participating got doused, and baseball in Seattle died. Our ship went down, too.

"Anyway, Mr. Fitzgerald had a welcome party for all of us in April, after things had settled down a bit. Just to give you a clue how inexperienced I was, they were passing around hors d'oeuvres and one was raw ground beef... and I thought it was a mistake, they forgot to cook it. I literally had to ask Bill Sears if they made a mistake, and he laughed and said, 'No, it's what they call a cannibal sandwich here in Milwaukee.' Of course, it was my first experience with steak tartare, raw minced beef with rye bread, onion, pepper, and other seasonings.

"Thinking back, oh my God, was I a babe in the woods."

Bob eventually came to know all the owners, well enough, in fact, that later one owner's wife on occasion babysat Bob's daughter. He also eventually started reporting to the board composed of the owners. "I used to have dreams about errors in the report somewhere; I would wander through numbers in my dreams, as if I were wandering through corn fields. I'd wake up and write something down from the dream. The next morning I'd wake up and go through that part of the report again, and I'll be damned if I didn't find something almost every time. It was weird."

Schoenbachler later unknowingly became involved in ownership-related family issues of a different kind. "Bud never told me about his personal life, he appeared to keep that to himself pretty much. But the rumor around the ballpark was that both Bud and his brother were in Jewish marriages arranged by their parents, and Bud, in particular, had grown unhappy over the years."

Selig had gotten married in the early 1950s, when many Jewish marriages were, if not arranged, then "highly encouraged."

Selig had known Sue Steinman, who worked in the team's public relations department, for a long time. She was close to the game, as involved as he was in the day-to-day life of baseball. "It was clear to everyone that he had developed feelings for Sue. I really got to know her over time, she always treated me with respect, and we really got along."

Selig wanted his staff to interact with counterparts from other clubs to develop relationships that would help them learn new things. As a result of Schoenbachler's good rapport with Sue, he was asked by Selig to escort her to several of these events where the team was playing out of town.

"I would drop her off at the hotel where the owners would stay, and I would go to the hotel where the players and staff stayed."

After a few of these escort trips, Dick Hackett, Gabe Paul Jr., and a couple of other guys from the front office started calling me 'the beard' because I gave Sue and Bud cover. I was so young and fresh off the farm at the time that I had to ask them what a 'beard' was the first time I heard it."

Bud and his wife, Donna, divorced in 1976 after nineteen years of marriage, a little more than a year after Bob left Milwaukee. Donna, in court documents, claimed that Selig had been "unduly absenting yourself from the home of the parties . . . in pursuit of your baseball interest to the detriment of your marriage." She later stated that Selig "divorced me and married baseball."[3]

In 1977, a year after the divorce, Selig married Suzanne Steinman (known to club officials as Sue). They remain married as of this writing.

As Bob recalls, public embarrassment was one of the issues that most bothered Bud Selig, so of course he wanted to avoid that. "The maddest I ever saw Bud was the time he took Baseball Commissioner Bowie Kuhn and a couple of other club owners out to dinner. Bud picked up the tab, and his American Express card was declined. He was both shocked and livid, and I know that because he personally called me in the middle of the night, mad as hell, asking me to explain to him why his card had been declined. I called American Express the next morning, they researched it, and they were embarrassed to tell us that they had sent incorrect cards not only for Bud, but for the entire management team. They had to replace them all. It was embarrassing and frustrating at the time, but thinking back now, I'm not so upset about it. That's because much later

Bowie Kuhn once told me 'You're getting fat.' To me, he acted like he was God's gift to baseball. Thinking back, I hope he had to pick up the bill that night."

Meanwhile, the "new" Milwaukee GM Marvin Milkes, who transitioned from Seattle, was evaluating his life direction and career security.

Milkes had Selig a bit over a barrel given the need for a rapid transition from Seattle to Milwaukee. He asked for and received from Milwaukee a two-year extension on his contract.

"One suspects Bud Selig was not happy to have that particular relationship forced upon him, either, but he did it to provide stability and prevent disruption at the start of the first 1970 Milwaukee season," Bob recalled.

Marvin Milkes (left) with Bud Selig in Milwaukee in 1970. (Source: Historic Images Outlet)

Milkes made it through opening day and stumbled his way through the new season as well. Lew Matlin, one of Jim Kittilsby's first mentors in baseball administration, had accompanied Milkes to Milwaukee from Seattle. Lew was thought by some to be the "hand-holder" to Milkes that got him through his constant stressing out.

As the end of the year approached, a season in which the team won only one game more than Seattle had in the previous year, "Milkes immediately went nuts signing guys to new contracts, as usual without consulting or listening to others," Schoenbachler recalled. As the finance guy, he saw all the contracts.

Selig wanted to be fully in the loop on salaries and differences between the old and the upcoming salaries. He saw what was happening and asked for a report. Schoenbachler gave it to him, with a copy to Marvin Milkes. "I specifically gave Marvin a copy so he wouldn't think I was going around him, but he went ballistic that I'd given such a report to Selig. He chewed me out, yelling at the top of his voice, and said that from that moment on, I reported only to him."

Bill Sears, who agreed to come along to Milwaukee from Seattle to serve as public relations director during the transition, overheard Milkes laying into Bob, but he could not make out why.

"As I retreated from the yelling Marvin Milkes and walked by Sears's office, he asked, 'What the hell have you done?'

"I just shook my head as I went by Bill's office.

"Realizing I may be stuck with Milkes for several years on his extended contract, and having already experienced Milkes's dysfunction in Seattle, I left the office, got in my car, left the stadium, and drove over to Selig Ford, Bud's car dealership. I meet with Bud, who's got one of his twelve Coca-Colas a day on his desk, and announce that I'm resigning. It goes something like this: 'I can't take this shit from Milkes anymore; I appreciate the offer to stay, but I'm resigning and returning to Seattle.'"

Bud's quiet reply to Bob: "We're going to correct that situation with Milkes; that's confidential. Hang in there." Bud had already seen enough in year one, and he didn't like any of it. Milkes's behavior was becoming an embarrassment of its own.

Bob remembers Milkes's actions after the move being consistent with what he had seen in Seattle. "Milkes was a yeller and picked on people, and that act was already in play after just a short time in Milwaukee. In addition to intimidating staff, he'd also already raised hell with Dave Bristol, the team's field manager that Milkes himself hired after letting Schultz go. Nervous as hell about everything, he was constantly flying into random tantrums. He seemed unbalanced."

Gabe Paul Jr. was one of the staff who came over from Seattle to Milwaukee, and he in particular was one who appeared to avoid drama with Milkes or anyone else, for that matter. "His office was called the dungeon because it was a great place to hide out in the stadium. He stayed away from any conflict that would be going on in the main office. Over the years as people got fired or resigned from the club, Gabe had their nameplates with former title hanging in his office on the back of his door, called 'the Wall of Shame.' Not too many people knew about the door. There were times Gabe's favorite secretary may have also used the dungeon to soothe Gabe's nerves a bit."

Gabe's concern for staying out of office conflict may have been heightened by the experience of one Jack Hutchinson. Jack, who worked with Gabe, was shipped off to Visalia, California, to work for a low-level minor league club after it was found out that he was dating the beautiful daughter of Ed Fitzgerald, one of the owners. "Let's just say Ed didn't like anybody messing with his daughter and decided to use his influence."

Schoenbachler received a call from Selig within a week of meeting with him to tender his resignation. Said Selig: "You're coming with me tomorrow to Boston to see Joe Cronin, American League president. It's confidential, and I don't want anyone to know. I need approval from the league to terminate

Marvin Milkes and get out of Marvin's contract. I need you there as a third party to verify some of the behaviors."

Arriving in Boston, Bob accompanied Bud Selig to the office of Joe Cronin. "I think it was sometime in November," Bob recalls. As they were involved in early discussions, in barged Charlie Finley, not one to let social convention get in the way of a grand entrance. Finley, of course, asked what Selig was doing in town, "at which point the BS started to fly about why we're there."

The old bullshit grinder would have been working overtime right about then.

Finley, apparently satisfied with the answer he got, invited the men to lunch at Jimmy's on the Harbor, a high-end VIP hangout. They all agreed to make their way to Jimmy's.

Bob continued, "Charlie O., flamboyant as ever, orders sushi, not a common dish at the time, and makes a big deal of it. He chides Bud into giving it a try. I see Bud is having a hard time with it, trying to swallow with grace and not being very successful at it. Mr. Finley then offers me some."

Bob replied with some embarrassment: "If I eat that, I'm pretty sure I'll throw up." The memory of having to choke down a Caesar salad with anchovies on it in front of Phil Duffy at 13 Coins popped into his head.

Finley's response surprised everyone at the table: "I respect you for that answer," he said, smiling.

"Later during lunch, Finley looked at me during the conversation and announced, 'Why don't you come and work for me? After I get back home, maybe we can discuss a job offer.' Not knowing for sure whether Finley is kidding or not, everyone chuckles. Even though we are there partly because I was so unhappy with Milkes, Bud intentionally misstates, 'Bob is very happy in Milwaukee,' the stories and small talk proceed, and lunch comes to its timely end. This allows Bud, me, and

Joe Cronin to get back to the issue at hand after returning to Cronin's office."

After returning to Milwaukee, and with the approval of the league, Bud Selig fired Marvin Milkes, to whom he had less than a year earlier given an extended contract.

In an interview years later, Bill Sears recalled how the firing played out in public. "During the winter holidays, we had a Christmas party for the ballpark people. Selig told me that we were going to fire Milkes, and to have a press release written up right away and get it out. I left the party, went back to my office, and got a press release out to the *Milwaukee Journal*. I guess Bud told Marvin directly."[4]

The *Milwaukee Journal* reported Milkes's departure as a resignation. Milkes said that due to "personal and business reasons, there was a pressing and immediate need for him to spend more time in the Los Angeles region." He was given the position of special assignment scout in California. Selig said the resignation came as a surprise, and temporarily he would share the GM duties with Bobby Mattick, director of player procurement and development; Dave Bristol, field manager; and Tommy Ferguson, traveling secretary. When asked if Milkes jumped or was pushed from the GM position, Selig stated the change had been made to the mutual benefit of both parties.[5]

Selig immediately hired Frank Lane, well known in the game, as general manager. In fact, office scuttlebutt had it that Lane was already holed up in the Pfister Hotel in Milwaukee. He got a phone call. "Marvin's gone." Over the Christmas holidays or shortly thereafter a contract was quickly worked out, and Lane was "officially" on board in January. Serious conversations had obviously taken place sometime earlier.

It was Milkes's last year in baseball; he never received another offer, or at least one to his liking.

Jim recalls, "My last contact with Milkes was the summer of 1971 after he left Milwaukee, and I was back at Pacific Lutheran University. He didn't get another baseball offer but decided to start up his own baseball administration school in Palm Springs. His idea was to offer advice to young people interested in a job in baseball administration, and to have him and his other baseball contacts come in and basically give tips and lectures on how to hook up with a team and what kind of jobs might be out there. There were few, if any, internships then like there are today. At least for a while it worked out, as he asked me, and some of his contacts with the California Angels and Los Angeles Dodgers to come in and talk. He didn't offer any pay, just airfare for my wife and I, a hotel room (cheap in the hundred-and-ten-degree heat of Palm Springs in the summer), and a food stipend. My wife and I decided to take him up on a free trip and week in Palm Springs, and I gave my class poolside in the evenings because it was so hot during the day. My recollection is that over time he had hundreds of young people come in, some from as far away as New York.

"I remember Marvin was still quite nervous and not very sociable; he didn't even present a class himself, just those of us he asked ended up being the presenters.

"I don't know if he asked other guest speakers to do a little something extra at any point, but he asked me to respond to the many dozens of letters he would get, often from wives or mothers sending in their son's resumes and asking Lew to keep them in mind if he learned of an opening. I always just wrote back and said, 'We'll keep the resume on file' and signed off as the assistant director of the school.

"Obviously, that 'send in a resume with a letter from your wife' idea was not an effective way to get in the game. It was all about contacts and networking. Even in today's game with lots of internships connected to colleges with sports administration programs, probably the best way to get a job in the game is to get an internship with one of the teams in the Arizona Fall League and start to develop relationships with people connected to all the teams."

Given what many described as his high level of constant stress, it was not a big surprise to learn that Milkes died of a heart attack in 1982 at the relatively young age of fifty-eight, found in bed in his weekend room at the Los Angeles Athletic Club. As his last job, Milkes was general manager of the Los Angeles Aztecs of the North American Soccer League. Ironically, he resigned shortly before the Aztecs folded their franchise.[6]

Unfortunately, Lew Matlin, closely linked to Milkes in Seattle prior to Milwaukee, was let go at the same time Milkes was. As far as anyone knew, it was the first time Matlin had ever been fired from a baseball administrative position, and he was completely taken aback. Having helped pull the fat out of the fire for Milkes on numerous occasions, Matlin likely felt he had served Milwaukee well. He also was a baseball trivia master, as was Bud Selig, and they had often traded trivia questions together, so he likely felt he had developed a good relationship with Bud.

There were rumors that Lew was so floored by the outcome, he left the office with tears in his eyes. "Many of us felt badly for him," Bob recalls.

Lew Matlin (seated) shown here in 1984 in his Detroit Tigers office with Detroit Tigers community relations director Vince Desmond. Matlin was Jim Kittilsby's first baseball mentor and administrative counterpart in Tacoma, Seattle, and Milwaukee. (Source: Historic Images Outlet)

Matlin, respected in the game, immediately got picked up by the Detroit Tigers in 1971, and he spent the rest of his career there. He was later described this way:

> He was passionate about baseball and all the people who served the game at the major and minor league levels. He was one of those colorful baseball characters known as well for his cigars, rumpled suits and interminably long hours at the park as he was for the non-stop yarns he could spin about players, games, and all things connected to baseball.
>
> "Lew was special and it's a shame that every fan didn't have a chance to meet him," said Dan Ewald, former *Detroit News* baseball

writer and public relations director for the Detroit Tigers. "He had a steel trap mind for facts, figures and every little anecdote that breathed life into the game."[7]

"New" general manager Frank Lane, by this time seventy-five years old, had already been general manager for four other teams and had acquired a reputation as "Trader Lane" and "Frantic Frank." By the end of his baseball career, he had made 414 transactions involving 690 players, some of them twice. But beyond his trading reputation, he was also known to be a hard worker, knowledgeable, and one with whom others could work. Bob agreed with that assessment:

"He was a perpetual motion machine, up early, up late, on the phone constantly, with a win-it-now attitude. Take-no-prisoners, fear-no-evil kind of guy. Bud Selig was impressed with his knowledge of baseball history, names, and statistics of almost every player he ever met. And Bud, too, was constantly on the phone developing relationships and telling stories throughout the league.

"Selig was great with baseball trivia; he listened to baseball all the time and talked baseball all the time. He was also in motion all the time, but that might also be because he drank a dozen or more Coca-Colas a day."

Bob remembers that he and Frank Lane hit it off immediately. "He was like a grandfather to me, I was twenty-three, he was seventy-five," Bob recalls. "But oh my God, could he swear. And he used to come in, sit down, and immediately start bitching and cussing about people randomly. It was like it was his favorite pastime, almost funny! I think part of it was a show to entertain baseball people. He was a hell of a hard worker, a tough guy, and a lot of fun, but boy, he was a ball of fire and a bit of a loose cannon. The difference was, he wasn't always nervous, always stressed out, or a basket case like Milkes seemed to be most of the time; and he certainly didn't stay holed up in his hotel room like Milkes. Frank Lane enjoyed the hell out of his job."

Frank Lane, circa 1971–1972. (Public Domain)

Bob's son is named Gregory Lane Schoenbachler, which is an indicator of how well Bob and Frank Lane got along and how much Lane meant to the rest of Bob's baseball career.

"The only guy I met in baseball more vocal with filthy language than Frank Lane was maybe the biggest filthy mouth and shortest traveling secretary in the history of baseball, Donald Davidson of the Atlanta Braves," Bob remembers. "I met Davidson later in my first Milwaukee year at a Major League accounting conference in Atlanta. He was what everyone called a midget in those days, not realizing that was a term disliked by dwarfs. He was probably always cussing because players or his administrative counterparts did things like get his room changed to the highest floors in a hotel so he couldn't reach the elevator buttons at the top. I once saw a couple of players pick him up and hang him from a coat hanger on a wall, and he couldn't get down. I think that may have been the longest string of filthy swear words I've heard to this day."

Almost immediately, back in Milwaukee, Lane came to Bob's defense on a key issue, much to Bob's surprise. It turns out that Frank Lane, long in the game, was still friends with one Charlie Finley, now of Oakland, with whom he had once had a major contract dispute, which kept Lane out of baseball for almost three years. Their dispute long settled, Finley called Frank and told him he was interested in talking to Bob about a job offer. Finley had apparently raised the issue with Bud Selig again, and Bud had denied Finley permission to talk with Bob. Finley was trying the back-door method, using Frank Lane as his entry.

Upon hearing the story from Finley, Lane talked with Bob about it. Lane let loose with one of his by now infamous tirades, damn the torpedoes and full steam ahead. He was, after all, "a take-no-prisoners, fear-no-evil type of guy." Yelled Lane, "That goddamned [bigoted language about a Jewish person] won't let you talk to Finley?"

While the language was neither delicate nor appropriate, it wasn't bigotry; Lane was Jewish himself, and he and Selig got along. It was just Frank Lane being his intentionally dramatic, loud, and blasphemous self. Bob recalls, "I explained to Frank that I didn't think Bud could keep me from talking to Finley because I didn't have a contract, and Frank agreed."

Bob came to Milwaukee, as did his fellow workers, not knowing exactly how things would play out. Bob eventually received a new title, but never did receive a contract and not much of a raise. In fact, office personnel rarely received contracts.

With Lane's full support and encouragement, Bob immediately went to talk with "Budget Bud" Selig. Bud and Bob had actually had a small conversation about the same issue in the airplane on the way back from the meeting with Joe Cronin about Marvin Milkes, in which Finley injected himself as a surprise guest and first suggested a job offer to Bob.

"On the way back on the plane, I said to Bud something like, 'That was interesting that Mr. Finley offered me a job right in front of you.'"

Bud's reply was a simple but serious one: "You don't want to work for Charlie Finley. He's truly a loose cannon among the owners."

"I think I responded with a smile, but only half kiddingly, 'Yeah, but he might give me a lot more money.' Bud and I both knew that the West Coast was where I was from and therefore had a natural attraction. At that point I think we dropped the subject and moved on to something else."

But now, with another contact by Finley, Bob was back in Bud's office about the same issue. Bud was alone. Bob walked right in.

"Bud, I understand that Mr. Finley would like to talk with me about a job with him back on the West Coast, and you wouldn't let him. Why not?"

Bud hesitated for a moment, then said, "I won't let Charlie talk with you; that's tampering."

Bob replied, "How can it be tampering? I don't have a contract."

Bud hesitated again, then continued the discussion. He seemed to be searching for what might convince Bob to forgo the conversation with Finley.

After a brief discussion, Bud offered, "Here's what I can do for you. I can give you an immediate raise of three thousand dollars for the 1971 fiscal year. Will that work?"

"Oh, I think that will work" was Bob's happy response. "It's an honor to be asked by Mr. Finley, but this will work even better." Bob agreed to forget about Charlie Finley, and the meeting quickly ended, with all parties satisfied except perhaps Charlie Finley back in Oakland.

Bud was true to his word, arranging an immediate $3,000 raise, and from that point on, Bob's raises were more systematic and routine. At the end of the next year, Bob received a $3,000 raise into the 1972 year, and an additional raise of $6,000 for taking on additional financial duties with an expanding new arm of the organization run by Gabe Paul Jr. having to do with year-round events. Bob raised the issue himself on the $6,000 raise, having been given the new financial oversight responsibilities and also having confidence at this point that Bud would give him a fair hearing.

Charlie Finley had a major hand in ending the franchise for which Bob worked in Seattle by moving Finley's team from Kansas City to Oakland. He forced Seattle into a team before they were prepared, and would have cost Bob his job and career had he not been able to move to Milwaukee. Yet, ironically, Finley ended up peripherally and unintentionally assisting Bob in obtaining $12,000 in raises over a relatively short period of time.

First, Finley's request to talk to Bob forced the Bob and Bud "meeting of the minds" on Bob's value to Milwaukee and to Bud. And second, that meeting and the positive result further built confidence in Bob that Bud would talk with him, hear him, and treat him fairly. Bob did not hesitate much the next time he felt he had a good case to make. True, the raises were phased in over twenty-four months at the end of Bob's first and second years, but in 1970, $12,000 over that space of time was far from small change. In 2020 dollars, that's about an $81,000 raise in a little over two years.

"For being in baseball for such a short period of time and being so young, it truly was an honor that Mr. Finley wanted to talk to me about a job, but I was really happy in Milwaukee and with my improving relationship with Bud. I probably wouldn't have taken a job in Oakland anyway."

On the other hand, the A's went on to win three World Series shortly after, from which Bob would have received three World Series rings. As Yogi Berra would say, "It ain't over till it's over." Win some, lose some. Although, to be fair, office personnel did not receive World Series shares of playoff revenue as the players did.

At the same time, Bob was now somewhat of a right-hand man and confidante to a person later to become the commissioner of all of baseball.

"Bud and I were developing a trusting relationship, which was nice, but even soon after giving me a raise, he still stayed focused on me and everyone else getting stuff done, and making sure the team came first. That winter, 1971, going into my second year, we had a big snowstorm. Seattle, while often wet, rarely has snow, and when we do, everyone stays home. Seattle often didn't have the snow equipment to quickly service the entire area. So, in Milwaukee on this very snowy day, I instinctively stayed home. My phone rang. It was Bud, in at work. He wanted to know where I was. Of course, I told him I stayed home because it was snowing heavily. He firmly told me, 'Well, here in Milwaukee if it's snowing, you still go to work. Invest in some snow tires.' I went to work. And I got some snow tires.

"A bit later in 1971, I bought a home in Waukesha, a few miles outside of Milwaukee. While traveling to work, I would pass the small Waukesha airport. My dad was a pilot, and I used to love flying with him, so it was a great memory. I was also looking for something to take my head out of baseball and finance books, to give me a chance to relieve stress after two solid years of tough franchise start-ups for the Pilots and the Brewers. Gabe Paul Jr. was also a Vietnam veteran who flew helicopters, and he had taken me up a couple of times, so my interest in flying was really rekindled. I decided to stop by the airport and check on the cost of lessons. At some point, I was determined to learn to fly. Fast-forward, and about twenty-four months later I was in the air with an instructor almost every other morning, very early, before landing and heading for work.

"Bud heard I was flying and asked to talk with me. 'Bob, I want you to stop flying. You are a corporate officer now, and if something were to happen to you, we'd be in trouble because you are the guy that knows all the numbers.'

"I was a bit shocked by the request, probably first because flying was not at all fearful for me, since my dad was a pilot and I had flown with him often when younger. I didn't have the same sense of danger that Bud or others might have in piloting a plane. But secondly, I was doing this on my own time. The two of us got into a discussion about it, my explaining that it was an important stress reliever for me, that I was familiar with flying from my dad's being a pilot, and finally, it seemed to me that what I did on my own time was my business.

"As always, Bud gave me a fair hearing. He finally agreed that I could go ahead and continue flying, with one caveat, 'You can't be flying with anybody else from the club, players included, because that increases the risk for the club.' I agreed, continued my lessons, and got my license in October 1973.

"The problem is, when some of the other administrators heard I'd gotten my license, several of them immediately got together and insisted I take them for a ride. Our VP and traveling secretary, Tommy Ferguson, our equipment manager, Bobby Sullivan, and our club trainer, Curt Rayer hauled me off to the airport and talked me into flying to Lake Geneva,

Wisconsin, about twenty minutes by air. What was in Lake Geneva that had everyone so anxious to go there? The Playboy Club, where we promptly spent the afternoon.

"As far as I know, Bud never found out. I suspect he would have had me on the phone again, or in his office, if he had."

14

Deeper Team Depth Buys Milwaukee Time (and More)

Budget Bud knew his numbers and didn't waste his money, and he had a lot more to work with than the Seattle Pilots had.

To begin with, Milwaukee had a stadium that wasn't completely falling apart. While old, it had held a major league team as recently as 1965. And instead of paying rent to the city, which the Pilots were required to do for a dilapidated stadium barely worthy of a minor league team, much less a major league team, Milwaukee only paid one dollar a year for rent. That deal was in place until Milwaukee reached one million in attendance, so for multiple years they paid basically nothing for the stadium.

Second, Bud and the Brewers were backed by a large team of corporate leaders, investing as individuals, including Robert Uihlein Jr. of the Joseph Schlitz Brewing Company, Oscar Mayer Jr., Ralph Evinrude of Evinrude Boat Motors, Edmund Fitzgerald of Cutler-Hammer, and Eddie Foote from Elmer, New Jersey.

Few, if any, of Seattle's major corporate leaders had shown interest in making sure the Pilots were a successful franchise and community asset. Or if they did, they were either not willing or not able to put money where their interest was.

By contrast, in Milwaukee in 1971 and again in 1972, as bleak attendance figures rolled in, Bob and Bud saw the bad news. The first year, 1970, was acceptable given the late start-up, but 1971 and 1972 were very disappointing. Shaking his head, but with a smile, Bob recalled, "By 1972 we were pinching pennies so tightly we were even running out of baseballs, and the tension was really high. I remember Tommy Ferguson, now traveling secretary for the club, screaming, 'We can't run out of baseballs! How the hell do you play baseball without baseballs!'

"At the time, it seemed like an impending disaster.

"Each time we got into a budget squeeze, Bud asked me how much we needed. I dug into the numbers, gave him a figure, and we reported the bad news to the board of owners each time. We talked our way through it, and the investors came through with more cash." The investors were hanging in there, committed to making it through the hard times.

When Bob met investor and owner Ralph Evinrude in Milwaukee, Bob asked Evinrude why he was an investor in the Brewers baseball franchise. Evinrude replied, "This city has been very good to me in all my years; it's my way to repay the city."

Bob remembers, "One lesson I learned was how budget issues were so much more routinely and calmly handled in Milwaukee, as compared to the one year in Seattle. Perhaps that's because the Seattle venture was so shaky right from the start, with the stadium not ready, and people in important positions being fired on opening day . . . actually, even before opening, counting Phil Duffy . . . and attendance so obviously low. Everyone knew attendance was about the only real revenue we had in Seattle, so that had people on a tightrope. I think that set a tone, everyone realizing things were very tight and tense. We were scrambling every single day.

"In Milwaukee, the staffing overall was more stable and compartmentalized, and we were able to pretty quickly establish written financial procedures for review of expenses by the department heads. The check-signing procedures went through me, and then Bud, for double signatures. In Seattle, because we were just learning and scrambling, all of our written procedures weren't yet well developed.

"The difference was really brought home to me when I was signing checks from expense reports of the Milwaukee staff while talking on the phone with a finance guy from another team, I think it was Minnesota. As I'm leafing through the paperwork and signing checks and we're shooting the bull, he happens to mention something like, 'I think one of our scouts took one of your scouts out to dinner recently.' Just seconds earlier, I had signed the check for that very scout of ours about whom he was speaking. It was a one-in-a-million chance he would comment on it right after I'd just signed the scout's check. 'You won't believe this, but I just signed that check for our scout,' I told him. 'I see our guy splurged a little and picked up the tab.'

"'No,' he replied, '*our* guy picked up the tab.' Stunned, I replied, 'Holy shit! How much does your guy say he paid?' I don't recall the amount now, but both guys turned in an expense for the same amount, both saying they had paid for the other guy. At least one of our scouts was double-dipping on his expense account. I took the check back to the scouting department and basically said, 'Hey, we've got a bit of a problem here.' They took care of it. And nobody complained. Having set and written procedures made it a simple transaction in Milwaukee. In Seattle's one and only year, we were developing procedures on the run; getting them established as 'completely routine' was probably a year away . . . a year we never got to."

Another advantage in Milwaukee: Bud Selig was adamant about his team being on the leading edge of technology, although he wasn't into technology much personally. He backed that up by supporting the idea of Bob learning programming from the company supplying the Milwaukee Brewers computer service. Remember, this was over a decade before Microsoft even went public.

Bob and Tony Siegle, who worked in minor league player evaluation for the Brewers, began to employ a mainframe at IBM in Cleveland to help determine a value of a player through a computer program. Years later, the MLB Scouting Bureau for all of baseball would be using the concept of computer programming and some of the algorithms that Bob and Tony helped to establish. "Several years after our work, I remember meeting Jim Wilson, who by then was directing the MLB Scouting Bureau." Jim Wilson and Bob were familiar with one another, as Wilson was general manager of the Brewers for a couple of years after Frank Lane departed. "Jim told me they were using some of our early analysis and trying to upgrade it further to make player analysis a more exact process. I thought that was a heck of a compliment."

In essence, Bob and Tony's early work helped change the way players were scouted and evaluated by all of baseball, some of the very preliminary work in what is now called analytics.

Bob knew he was now in a much healthier business setting in Milwaukee than he had been in Seattle. The Milwaukee business-community "backup players" had a lot more baseball interest, a bigger commitment to the team's success, and a lot more "connected" corporate talent.

That being said, it was also true that the actual baseball team coming to Milwaukee from Seattle was not loaded with talent.

The team that left Milwaukee for Atlanta carried with it a talented outfielder named Henry "Hammerin' Hank" Aaron, who would later break Babe Ruth's all-time home run record. Another future Hall of Fame player, Eddie Mathews, held down third base.

In addition, they had been the team of Warren Spahn, the winningest left-handed pitcher in all of baseball history, whom Bob had met in Seattle, introduced to him by the one and only roommate of Babe Ruth, Jimmie Reese, a coach with Seattle at the time. Spahn had nine twenty-win seasons in Milwaukee, and his career numbers included a 3.09 earned run average in 5,243 innings pitched, with a 1.19 WHIP. As the leader of a thin pitching staff for part of his time in Milwaukee, he was invaluable, and "Spahn and Sain and pray for rain" became a well-known saying. In often overcast and misty Seattle, those prayers would have been more often answered than in Milwaukee. Spahn's last season in Milwaukee was 1964, not that long before the return of the Brewers in 1970.

Given the high caliber of players in their recent past, Milwaukee fans were not likely going to flock to see a poor ball club, the remnants of the terrible Seattle Pilots.

Early on, Frank Lane and Bud Selig both knew the above was true, and Selig, having far more trust in Lane than he had in the departed Milkes, gave Lane authority to move whomever he needed to at the major league level. Frank flew into action, and by the end of the 1971 season, thirty-three of the original forty-man roster had been turned over by Trader Lane.

It didn't help much.

In Milkes's first and final 1970 season as GM, Milwaukee ended the season with a 65–97 record, thirty-three games out of first place, tied with Kansas City for fourth/fifth place in a six-team division. Only the Chicago White Sox were worse. In Lane's first season as GM, in 1971, Milwaukee ended the season with a 69–92 record, thirty-two games out of first place, dead last in a six-team division.

Embarrassingly, Bud Selig also realized that the fan turnout was not meeting expectations, similar to Seattle. They were beyond Seattle in their first year, but in 1971 fell closer to Seattle territory, whose attendance in the Pilots' agonizing only year was 677,944. Fan attendance in Milwaukee in their first year, 1970, was officially announced as 933,690. In Frank Lane's first season as GM, attendance plummeted to 731,531. In 1972 it dropped again, to 600,440, below the 1969 Seattle Pilots number by a healthy (or unhealthy) sum.

But Certified Bob, who should know, says actual paid attendance by fans themselves in Milwaukee in 1972 fell even farther below that of the Pilots in 1969. "In 1972, our third year and second in a row of major attendance decline, I made an off-the-cuff remark to our ticket manager, Dick Hackett, that 'at least we hit 600,000.' I was shocked when he replied, 'Well, thanks to Selig Ford we did.' Dick told me many tickets were purchased by Selig's own Ford dealership. Selig Ford purchased and then gave away just enough tickets to customers and friends to avoid the embarrassment of taking a team from Seattle, only to draw less than 600,000 fans a few short years later. But without Selig Ford's 'silent participation,' we would have been under the 600,000 number. Until my conversation with Dick, I was only aware that money was coming in consistent with our attendance at a bit over 600,000. I had no idea whatsoever that Selig Ford was basically buying tickets and boosting the attendance numbers, so you know it was not something he wanted public at the time. In any event, the American League only counted paid attendance, and they didn't care at all about who paid or why, so we technically did have paid attendance in 1972 of 600,440."

Ironically, while the early years' attendance numbers were awful, they hid a major strength of the new franchise.

Fortunately, the Brewers were not totally dependent on ticket income to keep the franchise afloat, as Seattle had been.

The Milwaukee team was tied tightly to Milwaukee insiders with deep pockets now, unlike Seattle. The Milwaukee group stepped up when they were called upon to do so. Milwaukee County was most accommodating with stadium rent. Small-business owners who were hurt badly by the Milwaukee Braves leaving for Atlanta were all behind the new Milwaukee team, with few exceptions. Radio and television and concession contracts were more valuable.

Jim Wilson, who came to Milwaukee as director of scouting and player development in 1971, took over as general manager in 1973, where he stayed for only two years before heading the MLB Scouting Bureau. "I remember Bud really didn't want to lose Jim; the rumor was that Bud even offered him a lifetime job if he would stay with Milwaukee."

The very first player Wilson drafted was future Hall of Fame player Robin Yount, who spent his entire career with Milwaukee. A few years later, after drafting future Hall of Fame player Paul Molitor in 1978, and with the help of thirty-nine home runs from Gorman Thomas, the Seattle Pilots' second pick in the June 1969 draft, Milwaukee went on to appear in the World Series in 1982, losing in seven games to St. Louis.

The following year, they drew nearly 2.4 million fans.

EPILOGUE

Bob Schoenbachler

Bob Schoenbachler (left) with Bud Selig in 2016. (Courtesy of Bob Schoenbachler)

Bob stayed with Milwaukee for nearly five years, leaving baseball and returning to the Northwest in the summer of 1974.

"When I realized I would like to do something out of baseball, it took me almost a year to resign, as I had one of the greatest jobs and worked for some of the greatest owners in baseball. Even my time in Seattle was tremendously exciting and challenging as a new professional, as chaotic as it was. I loved my job, but it wasn't fulfilling any longer. Maybe the challenge was gone.

"I resigned in early 1974, and it was one of the hardest things I had to do. Bud Selig was wonderful to me. I wanted to leave before the season started, but they didn't get a replacement for me and kept stalling. Because I had announced my resignation in early 1974, by the time the season started I had lost interest and wanted to move on to my next career, whatever it may be. Finally, I just had to put pressure on Bud that I was going to leave June 1. Bud said, 'But we don't have anyone to replace you.' I replied, 'I don't care if you don't have anyone to replace me. I'm leaving June 1.' It was over after that.

"After it was announced that I was leaving, I got offers from other sports clubs. One was with the World Football League team in Hawaii and again with the Oakland Athletics, but I knew I just wanted to go back to the Northwest and do something for myself, be my own boss.

"After arriving in Seattle, I had no job, my wife was pregnant with our third child, I had no idea what was next, but I took the leap. I was getting calls from people who wanted me to get involved in the purchase of the new Seattle expansion team (now the Seattle Mariners) but I knew I wanted to do something else.

"Dewey and Max Soriano, with whom I was still on very good terms, purchased a very small shipping company called Western Pioneer, which serviced western Alaska communities, and wanted me to go to work for them. They kept calling, but I resisted for months and then my money was starting to run out and I needed a job, so late 1974 I decided to take the job. It was half my baseball salary. I told them that I didn't know how long I would work for them, as I wanted to do something for myself.

"I found myself really enjoying the challenges in the maritime industries. After three months with the Sorianos, I resigned, and two associates and I started our own maritime company on a shoestring and prayer.

"We went into competition with the Sorianos with a small World War II freighter that almost bankrupted us all by itself, it needed so much repair. Then we lost fifty thousand dollars on our first voyage. And the Sorianos were very tough competitors. But we figured things out after we started accompanying the ship on trips.

"I loved doing business in Alaska, as everything was on a handshake, and if you didn't live up to your commitment you would be out of business. Curiously, the flying license I obtained while in Milwaukee was a big advantage in our business, as I could fly into places not easily traversed in Alaska. It was also a huge advantage to have potential business customers up in a plane for an hour or two, alone with them while we talked business.

"Over the years, things expanded and we got involved in tugs and barges, and won a contract to operate a ferry in Steilacoom, Washington, on the Puget Sound. In 1998 the company was purchased by Harley Marine, and we came out of that whole deal quite well.

"Ten years after leaving baseball, in 1984, I unexpectedly found myself testifying on behalf of the Milwaukee Brewers case with the IRS. The case involved the valuation of the purchase of the Seattle club by Bud Selig, and the depreciation of the owner-player contracts. The purchase price at the time was $10.8 million, $10.2 million for owner-player contracts, which Milwaukee had depreciated over five years, and $100,000 for equipment and $500,000 for franchise cost.

"Because I was involved on both sides, Seattle and Milwaukee, involving the value of player contracts, I testified for a full day."

Certified Bob to the end, even ten years later.

Bob continued, "All these years later, the IRS had challenged the $10.2 million player contracts that Seattle and Milwaukee had agreed upon and Milwaukee used in depreciation. The IRS contended that, instead, the $10.2 million was the franchise cost, nondepreciable, and the $500,000 franchise fees Milwaukee and Seattle had agreed upon should instead be the depreciable asset. Bud and other Milwaukee owners had already had to pay extra taxes because of that IRS interpretation. Bud decided to challenge the IRS position on franchise cost versus player contract cost in US District Court for the Eastern District of Wisconsin.

"I particularly remember one instance during the proceedings when the attorney kept asking me about one player in particular, who wasn't showing up on the Pilots balance sheet like all the others. The player was Gus Gil. When Pacific Northwest Sports, Inc., under the Sorianos, later to become the Pilots, purchased the Seattle Angels in 1968, one player, Gil, was included. At the time, the auditors placed that player's contract cost under 'Organization Cost' on the balance sheet. It was an unusual purchase arrangement. I don't remember all the contract and value details, but it seemed like the attorney wanted to know why Gil's contract with Seattle was not listed among the players like all the others, but when ownership was transitioned to Milwaukee, there was Gus Gil, listed with Milwaukee. He kept asking me about the Gil contract.

"Is it here? 'No.'"

This line of questioning continued for quite some time.

"Finally, he asked skeptically, 'Well, where is it, then?' thinking he had made his point, that we were somehow playing games about team value with Gil.

"In fact, Gus was a player the Pilots received well before the draft, as part of a purchase of a minor league franchise, unlike so many of the other players. So, unlike almost every other player, he was listed elsewhere, outside of the normal listings, which I then explained to the court. I'll always remember the attorney's surprise response. He looked at me with a slight smile, pointed his finger at me, and said, 'Touché.' At that point, I relaxed. Even ten years later, as sharp as that attorney really was, I felt like I knew more about the financial statements than he did.

"The auditors at the time of the Gus Gil purchase, and under unusual circumstances, were simply trying to place Gus

Gil in a correct category at the time, where he had remained until the sale of the Seattle franchise to Milwaukee."

This case turned out to have major consequences for other teams. As Bob says, "To make a long story short, Milwaukee won the case. The player contracts were considered the depreciable asset. Bud and the other Milwaukee owners received a substantial tax refund. Valuing the owner-player contracts as a depreciable asset in a sale became a precedent, which then facilitated the purchase of the Yankees from CBS."

It turns out that Bob Schoenbachler's knowledge and testimony in the way the Seattle Pilots valued their players' contracts at their purchase price, and the way Milwaukee valued their players' contracts that they purchased from Seattle, helped make a positive case for Milwaukee and other teams as they were sold to new owners over time.

The decision in this case was of tremendous value in helping to establish legal precedent for depreciating player value and bringing another level of clarity to baseball finance. With more clarity and certainty about their legal standing in depreciating contract value from the player's purchase price, ownership could be more confident in making financial decisions.

The same kind of impact can be said to have resulted from Bob and Tony Siegle's early computer work and statistical analysis of player skills and abilities. Their computer-assisted analysis helped to bring another level of detail to player evaluation and change the face of baseball scouting.

All this from a guy who entered the game at the age of nineteen never having seen a major league game or played high school baseball, and who had not yet earned an accounting degree. But by the age of twenty-three, Bob had overseen the complex financial details of starting up two brand-new Major League Baseball franchises a thousand miles apart.

Bob, now retired, resides in North Scottsdale, Arizona.

Jim Kittilsby

Jim Kittilsby, circa 2010. (Courtesy of Pacific Lutheran University)

Jim Kittilsby returned to the Northwest in July 1970, as planned. Pacific Lutheran University, his alma mater, was excited to get a Major League Baseball professional administrator as its assistant athletic director, baseball coach, sports information director, facilities manager, head of the athletic booster club, and sports ad salesman connected to local business all wrapped up into one. As he was with the Seattle Pilots, he was with PLU, serving effectively behind the scenes, juggling many responsibilities and titles.

In 1978 Kittilsby was named Puget Sound Athletic Administrator of the Year by the Tacoma *News Tribune*. As sports information director, he won three "best in the nation" awards for his recruiting books and media guides. He was elected to PLU's Athletics Hall of Fame in 2001 and the Tacoma/Pierce County, Washington Sports Hall of Fame in 2008.

Kittilsby retired from PLU in 1993. He, too, resides in Scottsdale, Arizona. He spends a lot of time watching baseball in the MLB spring training facilities all over the area, which now host fifteen major league teams. He has worked in the Arizona Fall League and for the World Baseball Classic.

The Sorianos

Twenty-one-year-old Dewey Soriano (left), in the fashionable hat, and younger brother Max, two of ten Soriano siblings, here in 1941, a quarter of a century before they brought Major League Baseball to Seattle for the first time. (Source: David Eskenazi Collection)

After baseball with the Pilots, Dewey Soriano and brother Max returned to their other love, the sea. Together they started a shipping company with a major focus on serving Alaska.

Soriano was heartbroken about losing the Pilots, according to his daughter. "That was his big dream, to bring major league baseball to Seattle, and it got away," she said. "To have his dream shattered like that, it hurt him. Someone once gave him Pilots memorabilia as a gift. He didn't want it. It was a sad memory for him."[1]

Dewey Soriano spoke to this issue himself in his 1994 interview with Mike Fuller of SeattlePilots.com:

> Fuller: "Do you regret that it didn't work out?"
> Soriano: "I regret it very much, but I've got to be a realist and I have to look at myself in the mirror and say I was, at least partially, responsible for it not working. I think as you go back to the original premise I had that baseball would not only survive, but it would flourish in Seattle, and I was too optimistic as to what are some of the ingredients that would cause it to do that. Looking back on it now, I was very naive."[2]

Dewey eventually became president of the Puget Sound Pilots, an organization responsible for maneuvering freighters and other large vessels entering and departing Puget Sound. In 1982, piloting a large freighter himself, Dewey hit a bridge. Rumors are that sales of Dewey on the Rocks skyrocketed.

Dewey Soriano died in 1998 at the age of seventy-eight; brother Max died in 2012 at the age of eighty-seven.

Seattle Baseball

While the Sorianos' effort to bring major league baseball to Seattle is most often thought of only in the context of the Pilots' mercurial and disastrous rise and fall in a single year, it is also true, and rarely credited, that the Soriano's focused work to help pass the Forward Thrust levy was instrumental in building the Kingdome. And the Kingdome, completed in 1976, enabled the award of the Seattle Mariners franchise, which in turn resulted in Ken Griffey Jr., Edgar Martinez, Ichiro Suzuki, Felix Hernandez, Alex Rodriguez, Randy Johnson, and many others.

There is a direct line that can be drawn from the Sorianos' successful work to maintain AAA baseball in Seattle to their work on Forward Thrust to obtain the Kingdome and the Pilots, and then to the Mariners. Without Forward Thrust and the Kingdome, the Mariners would not be in Seattle today. While the Seattle Pilots flamed out, the fire for a team continued to smolder until Seattle was awarded a replacement franchise, and for that the Sorianos should be given substantial credit. The Mariners truly are part of the Soriano legacy.

Since 1977, the year Seattle obtained its "replacement" MLB team after lawsuits were threatened and the issue of withdrawing the MLB antitrust exemption was again raised (this time by powerful senator Slade Gorton of Washington State), Seattle has never reached the World Series. They are now the only current major league team never to have played in a World Series. Some have speculated that the lack of a World Series appearance has something to do with either a *"Ball Four* curse" or a 1970 "bankruptcy curse." Fifty years is over. So is the curse. Things are looking up for Seattle.

Despite the lack of a World Series appearance, the Mariners have exceeded 3 million in annual attendance five times, the first being in 1997. In 2002, Seattle Mariners attendance was 3,540,482, which at the time was among the highest ten all-time attendance figures in baseball history.

The Mariners franchise, according to a 2019 *Forbes* magazine analysis, is now worth $1.575 billion, ranking fifteenth of thirty Major League Baseball franchises.

Since the move of the Pilots to Milwaukee in 1970, Milwaukee has exceeded 3 million in attendance three times, in 2008, 2009, and 2011.

The current value of the Milwaukee Brewers, purchased from Seattle for $10.8 million in 1969, is now $1.2 billion, ranking twenty-fourth of thirty teams, according to *Forbes* magazine.

Bud Selig

Bud Selig (Source: Brian McDermid/Reuters Pictures)

Bud Selig was named acting commissioner of Major League Baseball in 1992 and took the permanent title in 1998.

About Selig, Dave Sheinin wrote this in July 2014, on the eve of Selig's retirement:

> He finds himself thinking about history a lot these days, not so much the ancient minutiae he can famously recite from memory— the 1953 Milwaukee Braves starting lineup, for example, or the name of that one obscure pitcher who did that one amazing thing in that

one game so many years ago—but History, writ large. His own history. Baseball history. American history. By this point, they're all intertwined.

This is what happens when you're about to turn 80, as Bud Selig will at the end of the month, and each week seems to bring the death of another good friend or colleague. It's what happens when you are preparing to step down from the job you have held for 22 years, as Selig will Jan. 24, a job you have cherished and in many ways transformed. It's what happens when you have held a lifelong obsession with history and now are confronted with it at every turn as the weeks tick down.

"The nicest part of all this is I have great memories," Selig says. "It's a tough job, no question, and I have a lot of tough days. But it's a remarkable human experience."[3]

During his time with Milwaukee, Selig won seven Organization of the Year awards from Major League Baseball. On the other hand, Selig was part of the owners' collusion in 1985–1987. Fay Vincent, baseball commissioner during that period, says, "They rigged the signing of free agents. They got caught."[4] The owners had to pay damages to the players of $280 million.

As commissioner, Selig sought to remove two teams from the league, Minnesota and Montreal.[5] Some have suggested that Minnesota was a convenient target for contraction, as it meant Milwaukee would grab a huge share of that regional market. Selig and former Montreal owner Jeffrey Loria were sued for racketeering and conspiring to defraud the Expos minority owners.[6] The case eventually went to arbitration and was settled out of court. The Expos eventually moved to Washington, DC, and Minnesota remained in Minneapolis.

Selig also served as commissioner during what is now known as the "steroid era," a period during which steroid use among players created massive increases in home runs, a resurgence of interest in the game hyped by MLB marketing . . . and much larger profits for owners. A report commissioned by Selig himself stated that the commissioner's office, club owners, the Players Association, and the players were all remiss and shared "to some extent in the responsibility for the steroid era."[7] Selig was widely criticized for moving much too slowly on the issue. But it is also true that in 1994, years earlier, Selig and others had proposed testing programs to the Players Association, but that was resisted at the time.

Also during his tenure as acting commissioner and commissioner, 1992–2015, revenue sharing between rich and not-so-rich clubs was expanded, interleague play was initiated, the league's divisions were restructured, the wild-card playoff teams were added along with divisional playoffs, twenty new stadiums were built (mostly with public funding), and the administrative structure was streamlined, eliminating National League and American League presidents. All clubs are now valued at over $1 billion each, and MLB annual overall revenue has grown from about $1 billion total to $9 billion.

Selig is said to have put up $300,000 of his own money to purchase the Seattle Pilots and move them to Milwaukee in 1970.[8] He sold the team thirty-five years later for $223 million.

Bud Selig's net worth today is approximately $400 million.[9]

ACKNOWLEDGMENTS

I've loved baseball since I was a small kid watching my mom play third base in a women's league in Elsinore, California, marveling at the beautiful satin green she and her teammates wore. I don't honestly recall if there were lights for a night game then, or green grass on the infield or outfield, but my memory is a beautiful sea of green complementing the shimmer of her uniform, with the single thin, white stripe on the uniform pants echoed by the chalk down each baseline.

My grandfather, Stanford Brooks—my mom's dad—also played ball. He was a minor league player in the Brooklyn Dodgers system in 1916. His career lasted only one year after he was beaned by an inside pitch. He got well just in time to serve during World War I. He attended the best baseball game I ever played in the summer of 1964.

I lost my dad to debilitating mental illness when I was eight, but the memories of playing catch with him as a six- and seven-year-old, lined up in our dirt driveway and tossing a ball back and forth, is a wonderful memory of him, healthy and happy, that will never fade.

Baseball was also an organizing element in my life with my two younger brothers, as our family struggled without a dad after he became ill. Every summer we spent time on a baseball field or in our yard, the game serving as a way to find joy and build camaraderie. Our summer in Corona, California, as late arrivals thrown together on a Little League team with other stragglers, remains one of my fondest childhood memories. Despite our age differences, we played together on the same rag-tag team and came in second place in the league, and not a distant second. We were tough and resilient.

I tried to create that same magic with my own kids, Ethan and Travis, as they grew up. Both of them are near forty now, yet one of their annual traditions remains buying boxes of baseball cards for the new year, opening them together and sharing their rookie finds. Both share my affinity for Mariners baseball.

Baseball even helped bring my wife and my mom closer; my mom was an athlete, a ballplayer, and a coach. My wife, only five feet tall, didn't participate in sports. So, my mom joined me in teaching Alvarita the game of baseball, which she now both understands and enjoys.

In short, my first thank-you goes to baseball itself. It's been far more than a game to me, and every game I attend reminds me of how much bigger it really is, as memories of my family play out as the innings pass.

Since baseball has been such a consistent element in my life, I often find myself in baseball conversations. And that's how I met Bob Schoenbachler, who was telling funny baseball stories at a dinner table in Africa with a small tour group. That conversation turned into this book. So, of course my next thanks most certainly must go to Bob Schoenbachler and Jim Kittilsby for the many hours we spent together talking and remembering, laughing, and correcting the many stories they shared about their time with the Seattle Pilots and Milwaukee Brewers. They arrived in Seattle with the Pilots by completely different paths, but ended up as lifelong friends, affirming once again the universal but mysterious special something that makes being on a team together unique.

Speaking of a team, two of my most important teammates in writing this book were Dr. Jerry Stringer and Marion

ACKNOWLEDGMENTS

Woyvodich, both of whom did yeoman's work in early review and editing. Trying to weave together a story with so many intersecting personalities and timelines is no easy task, and to the degree that this is a coherent work, they deserve much of the credit. And to the degree that it is not, that's on me. Likewise, a thank-you to the staff at Girl Friday Productions, in particular Sara Addicott, Georgie Hockett, and others behind the scenes who hand-carried me through the entire publication process even as the coronavirus raged.

I'd like to give a special shout-out to my younger son, Travis, an architect and artist, who designed the logo for Persistence Press, to my oldest son and computer genius, Ethan, who assisted in social media marketing and optimization, and finally to my patient and thoughtful wife, Alvarita. She watched me struggle to write a manuscript on early childhood development over two years only to see me take on *Inside Pitch* for another two. And without her technical assistance, I might still be unsuccessfully trying to print out the first draft pages of the manuscript.

Thanks also to Mikal Thomsen, current principal owner of the Tacoma Rainiers AAA team and a longtime friend who read an early draft. He encouraged me to continue the effort, suggested some useful insights, and provided that little bit of extra motivation that always comes in handy when you think you hit a wall or bit off more than you can chew. He, too, assisted in marketing the book, putting me in touch with some key people along the way.

And finally, we probably all owe a debt of gratitude to the late Jim Bouton, author of *Ball Four*. *Ball Four* was an eye-opening breakthrough book that forever memorialized the one-year Seattle Pilots in baseball history, much to the consternation of many in baseball at the time, and much to the enjoyment of most baseball fans who have read it or will read it. Far from just a baseball book, it's an inside look at the human condition from a ballplayer's perspective in 1969. Selected by the New York Public Library as one of the Books of the Century, it was the only book with a sports theme to be listed. If you haven't read it, you should.

Without all of the above, *Inside Pitch* would not have happened.

NOTES

CHAPTER 4

1 Larry Stone, "Edo Vanni Is the Dean of Seattle Baseball," *Seattle Times*, February 13, 2005, https://www.seattletimes.com/sports/edo-vanni-is-the-dean-of-seattle-baseball/.
2 Dan Raley, "Edo Vanni, 1918–2007: As Player, Manager, Promoter, He Was 100 Percent Baseball," *Seattle Post-Intelligencer*, April 30, 2007, https://www.seattlepi.com/sports/baseball/article/Edo-Vanni-1918-2007-As-player-manager-1235888.php.
3 Larry Stone, "Edo Vanni Is the Dean of Seattle Baseball," *Seattle Times*, February 13, 2005, https://www.seattletimes.com/sports/edo-vanni-is-the-dean-of-seattle-baseball/.
4 ESPN Automated Newswire, "Edo Vanni, Last Member of Original Seattle Rainiers, Dead at 89," Associated Press, May 1, 2007, http://www.espn.com/espn/wire/_/section/mlb/id/2854919.

CHAPTER 6

1 Dan Raley, "Where Are They Now: Bill Sears," *Seattle Post-Intelligencer*, April 24, 2007, https://www.seattlepi.com/sports/article/Where-Are-They-Now-Bill-Sears-tireless-1235308.php.

CHAPTER 7

1 "Gene Autry," Hollywood Star Walk, accessed March 23, 2020,

http://projects.latimes.com/hollywood/star-walk/gene-autry/.
2. "How Singing Cowboy Gene Autry Changed Country Music," Wide Open Country, accessed March 23, 2020, https://www.wideopencountry.com/how-singing-cowboy-gene-autry-changed-country-music/.
3. Bill Ruchlman, "Fans Admired the Ambitious Gene Autry," Daily Break, *Virginian-Pilot*, June 3, 2007, E-8.
4. "Review: Public Cowboy No. 1, The Life and Times of Gene Autry," Nous American (blog), April 12, 2007, https://sixthcolumn.typepad.com/nous_american/2007/04/review_public_c.html.

CHAPTER 8

1. Max Soriano, interview by Mike Fuller, seattlepilots.com, accessed March 23, 2020, http://www.seattlepilots.com/msoriano_int.html.
2. "History," seattlepilots.com, accessed March 23, 2020, http://www.seattlepilots.com/histindx.html.

CHAPTER 9

1. Amanda Lane, "How the Seattle Pilots Saved Lou Piniella's Baseball Career," Lookout Landing (blog), June 21, 2019, https://www.lookoutlanding.com/2019/6/21/18700246/how-the-seattle-pilots-saved-lou-piniellas-baseball-career.
2. Jim Bouton, *Ball Four: The Final Pitch* (Nashville, TN: Turner Publishing Company, 2014), 73.
3. Bruce Markusen, "Pound Some Budweiser: The Colorful Career of Joe Schultz," Vintage Detroit, August 24, 2014, https://www.vintagedetroit.com/blog/2014/08/24/pound-budweiser-colorful-career-joe-schultz-briefly-manager-tigers/.
4. Greg Johns, "Clubhouse Manager Genzale Retires after 37 Years," MLB.com, March 29, 2013, https://www.mlb.com/news/mariners-longest-tenured-employee-henry-genzale-retires-after-37-years/c-43494522.

5 Kenneth Hogan, *The 1969 Seattle Pilots* (Jefferson, NC: McFarland, 2007), 173.
6 Jim Bouton, *Ball Four: The Final Pitch* (Nashville, TN: Turner Publishing Company, 2014), 147.
7 Bill Mullins, "Build It and They Will Come," in *Becoming Big League: Seattle, the Pilots, and Stadium Politics* (Seattle: University of Washington Press, 2013).
8 Bill Sears, interview by Mike Fuller, seattlepilots.com, accessed March 23, 2020, http://www.seattlepilots.com/sears_int.html.
9 Larry Stone, "An Unstable Roller Coaster," *Seattle Times*, June 21, 2019, https://www.seattletimes.com/sports/mariners/it-was-a-one-season-roller-coaster-ride-at-sicks-stadium-50-years-later-the-pilots-remain-seattles-fun-fascination/.

CHAPTER 10

1 "Bill Sears, interview by Mike Fuller, seattlepilots.com, accessed March 23, 2020, http://www.seattlepilots.com/sears_int.html.
2 Max Soriano, interview by Mike Fuller, seattlepilots.com, accessed March 23, 2020, http://www.seattlepilots.com/msoriano_int.html.
3 Dan Raley, "Edo Vanni, 1918–2007: As Player, Manager, Promoter, He Was 100 Percent Baseball," *Seattle Post-Intelligencer*, April 30, 2007, https://www.seattlepi.com/sports/baseball/article/Edo-Vanni-1918-2007-As-player-manager-1235888.php.

CHAPTER 11

1 Dewey Soriano, interview by Mike Fuller, seattlepilots.com, accessed March 23, 2020, http://www.seattlepilots.com/dsoriano_int.html.
2 Leonard Koppett, "American League Weighs Shift of Pilots," *New York Times*, March 8, 1970, https://www.nytimes.com/1970/03/08/archives/american-league-weighs-shift-of-pilots-to-milwaukee-before-seasons.html.

3   Sidney Volinn, interview by Mike Fuller, seattlepilots.com, accessed March 23, 2020, http://www.seattlepilots.com/volinn_int.html.
4   Larry Stone, "Edo Vanni Is the Dean of Seattle Baseball," *Seattle Times*, February 13, 2005, https://www.seattletimes.com/sports/edo-vanni-is-the-dean-of-seattle-baseball/.

CHAPTER 12

1   "Baltimore Orioles Team History & Encyclopedia," baseball-reference.com, accessed March 23, 2020, https://www.baseball-reference.com/teams/BAL/index.shtml.

CHAPTER 13

1   "Allan Huber 'Bud' Selig," Encyclopedia of Milwaukee, accessed March 23, 2020, https://emke.uwm.edu/entry/allan-huber-bud-selig/; David Walstein, "Bud Selig, Apostle for Equity," *New York Times*, December 4, 2016, https://www.nytimes.com/2016/12/04/sports/baseball/bud-selig-an-apostle-for-equity-reaches-hall-of-fame.html.
2   "SS Edmund Fitzgerald," Wikipedia, accessed March 23, 2020, https://en.wikipedia.org/wiki/SS_Edmund_Fitzgerald.
3   Ben Reiter, "For Love or Money," *Sports Illustrated*, October 24, 2014, https://vault.si.com/vault/2014/10/20/for-love-and-money; Andrew Zimbalist, *In the Best Interests of Baseball? The Revolutionary Reign of Bud Selig* (Hoboken, NJ: John Wiley, 2006), 123.
4   Kenneth Hogan, *The 1969 Seattle Pilots* (Jefferson, NC: McFarland, 2007), 176.
5   Chris Zantow, "It Was 45 Years Ago Today—Milwaukee Brewers Research," Chris Zantow (blog), accessed March 23, 2020, https://chriszantowauthor.com/2015/12/17/it-was-45-years-ago-today-milwaukee-brewers-research/.
6   Obituary of Marvin Milkes, *New York Times*, February 2, 1982,

https://timesmachine.nytimes.com/timesmachine/1982/02/02/161988.html.
7. "Lewis Matlin," Dignity Memorial, accessed March 23, 2020, https://www.dignitymemorial.com/obituaries/st-clair-shores-mi/lewis-matlin-7689796.

EPILOGUE

1. Larry Stone, "An Unstable Roller Coaster," *Seattle Times*, June 21, 2019, https://www.seattletimes.com/sports/mariners/it-was-a-one-season-roller-coaster-ride-at-sicks-stadium-50-years-later-the-pilots-remain-seattles-fun-fascination/.
2. Dewey Soriano, interview by Mike Fuller, seattlepilots.com, accessed March 23, 2020, http://www.seattlepilots.com/dsoriano_int.html.
3. Dave Sheinin, "Bud Selig Leaves a Complex Legacy," *Washington Post*, July 13, 2014, https://www.washingtonpost.com/sports/nationals/bud-selig-leaves-a-complex-legacy/2014/07/11/37106a52-0764-11e4-9ae6-0519a2bd5dfa_story.html.
4. "Fay Vincent," Business of Baseball, SABR, accessed March 23, 2020, https://web.archive.org/web/20070202231828/http://www.businessofbaseball.com/vincent_interview.htm.
5. David Schoenfeld, "Still 30 Teams: Contraction Timeline," ESPN, accessed March 23, 2020, http://assets.espn.go.com/mlb/s/2002/0205/1323230.html.
6. Francie Grace, "Racketeering Suit Names Baseball Execs," *CBS News*, July 17, 2002, https://www.cbsnews.com/news/racketeering-suit-names-baseball-execs/.
7. George J. Mitchell, *Report to the Commissioner of Baseball of an Independent Investigation into the Illegal Use of Steroids and Other Performance Enhancing Substances by Players in Major League Baseball*, December 13, 2007, 310–11, http://mlb.mlb.com/mlb/news/mitchell/index.jsp.
8. Eben Novy-Williams, "Bud Selig Was Baseball's Great Hero,

Says Bud Selig," *Bloomberg Business Week*, July 9, 2019, https://www.bloomberg.com/news/articles/2019-07-09/bud-selig-book-review-he-s-mlb-baseball-s-hero-in-new-memoir.

9 "Bud Selig Net Worth," Celebrity Net Worth, accessed March 23, 2020, https://www.celebritynetworth.com/richest-athletes/richest-baseball/bud-selig-net-worth/.

ABOUT THE AUTHOR

While touring southern Africa, Allen found himself at a dinner table listening to funny stories from the former CFO of the Seattle Pilots, and with that, *Inside Pitch* was off and running.

Allen is a lifelong baseball fan who was living in California in the summer of 1958 when the new Los Angeles Dodgers moved from Brooklyn to LA. There, he began collecting baseball cards, never able to track down the card of Charlie Neal, second baseman for the Dodgers. Nearly sixty years later, his son found the card on eBay and surprised him with it at Christmas. Yes, he cried.

A Little League all-star at multiple positions and a frontline third baseman as a teenager in summer ball, Allen was a member of two county championship teams. His "storied career" in baseball ended at the age of eighteen as college called. He never saw a Pilots ball game, as the Pilots bounded to Milwaukee in 1970, and Allen went off to see new worlds with Uncle Sam.

In 1986, he became a rookie member of the oldest fantasy baseball league in the United States west of the Mississippi River. He's traveled to spring training in Arizona annually since 1986.

Married to Alvarita, his wife of over fifty years, they have two sons, both of whom played Little League ball, both of whom were coached at one time by Dad, and both of whom are Seattle Mariners fans.

Allen holds a BA in journalism from Eastern Washington, an MA in interpersonal communication from Ohio University, and an MA and a doctorate in public administration from the University of Southern California. He's worked in upper management and executive levels in the higher education, government, and nonprofit sectors and has founded and owned two small businesses.

Made in the USA
Monee, IL
10 June 2020

33158538R00104